F

Chocolate
for a Woman's
Soul

77 Stories to Feed Your Spirit
and Warm Your Heart

Kay Allenbaugh

A FIRESIDE BOOK
Published by Simon & Schuster

Chocolate

for a Woman's

Soul

FIRESIDE
Rockefeller Center
1230 Avenue of the Americas
New York, NY 10020

Copyright © 1997 by Kay Allenbaugh
All rights reserved,
including the right of reproduction
in whole or in part in any form.

FIRESIDE and colophon are registered trademarks
of Simon & Schuster Inc.

Permissions Acknowledgments appear on page 253.

Designed by Bonni Leon-Berman

Manufactured in the United States of America

15 16 17 18 19 20

Library of Congress Cataloging-in-Publication Data
Chocolate for a woman's soul : 77 stories to feed your spirit and warm your
heart / [compiled by] Kay Allenbaugh.
p. cm.
"A Fireside book."
1. Women—United States—Biography—Miscellanea. 2. Women—United
States—Conduct of life—Miscellanea. I. Allenbaugh, Kay.
HQ1412.C56 1997
305.4—dc21 96-51676
CIP
ISBN 0-684-83217-8

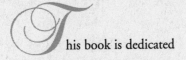his book is dedicated

to the memory of my mom,

whose playful spirit, unconditional love,

and encouragement

continue to bless me.

Contents

III

A Woman's Intuition

IV

Soaring Through Barriers

V

The Courage to Move On

VI

Crossroads

VII

Going the Distance

VIII

Go with Your Passion

A New Way of Being

Tenderness and Compassion

XI
Learning to Laugh at Ourselves

Introduction

*I*NSPIRATIONAL STORIES FEED OUR SOULS, LIFT OUR spirits, and warm our hearts. They help us to learn about ourselves and about life. I am honored that sixty-eight dynamic women have shared their favorite stories with me for *Chocolate for a Woman's Soul*. The writers are motivational speakers, spiritual leaders, consultants, therapists, best-selling authors, and their work has impacted thousands of people around the country. Who better to share inspirational stories than women who have devoted their careers to uplifting and encouraging others?

Their stories will tug at your emotions. Laughter, tears, reflective moments—all will surface as you share the magic and the miracles, the perfect timing and insights, these authors have experienced. Some stories will cause you to think about yourself, while others give you that boost you need to "go for" the next dream in your life.

The true stories in *Chocolate for a Woman's Soul* honor and celebrate a woman's true essence as wise, witty, courageous, powerful, soft, intuitive, nurturing, and playful. You will see yourself in many of these life experiences—and like what you see! Discover the common threads that each of us women experience in our life journey.

Why the title? Some things just go together. Chocolate and women have a natural bond. Women know that when all else fails, chocolate seems to help. Chocolate stimulates those "feel-good" endorphins in our bodies. Just like the rich and nurturing power of chocolate, the stories in *Chocolate for a Woman's Soul* will make your lives richer as they feed and nurture your souls.

Chocolate for a Woman's Soul has been a divinely inspired project, beginning with a strong message that I received unexpectedly one morning. While getting ready for my day, I felt the presence of a higher power. A voice seemed to whisper to me: "Write an inspirational book, *Women of Courage.*" The message commanded my attention and my energy. I took it literally, and I could not let go of it. I've since learned that writing the book had a lot to do with addressing my own courage issues.

The book I called "Women of Courage" didn't flow well, and my spirit began to wane. I became stuck and began to doubt myself. After all, I had never written a book! Who was I to undertake a project like this?

Only when I became true to myself and gave the book a title I loved and related to did it begin to flow effortlessly. I've since realized that I misinterpreted the original message. It was not: "Write an inspirational book, *Women of Courage,*" but rather: "Woman of courage, write an inspirational book." That changed things a lot! I discovered that God was partnering me and affirming that I am indeed a "woman of courage." Whenever I began to lose confidence, I'd remember the saying, "If you knew who was walking with you, how could you be afraid?"

I learned a lot about myself in writing and compiling these inspirational stories. My desire is that they affect your life as positively as they have affected mine. Savor the flavor as you explore each story in *Chocolate for a Woman's Soul.* Read the book cover to cover, or turn to a page randomly, knowing that the perfect story you need to read will reveal itself.

I

Finding Love in All the Right Places

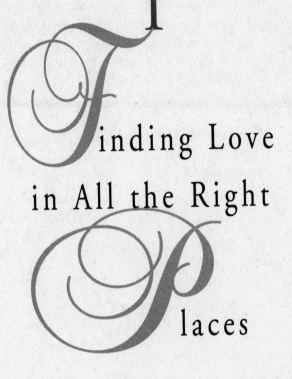

"For your ship to come in, you must first build a dock."

—Author unknown

How to Find Your Perfect Mate

DEAR ABBY ALWAYS SAID THAT HUSBANDS DON'T leave their wives for the other woman—mine did, and he married her. Suddenly single at thirty-eight, I looked for refuge in my work. Work helped me forget my painful divorce. I suppose I could have been interested in a partner, but for three years I was not attracted to anyone I met.

A friend of mine had just been to a workshop called "How to Find Your Perfect Mate." She cautioned that if I did not feel worthy enough to have my perfect partner, or did not believe wholeheartedly that he was on his way, this was not the time to go forward with the process.

She described the steps this way: 1. Make a long list of attributes you'd like in your partner. 2. Study that list carefully, and pare the number down to about fifteen qualities that are essential to you in a mate. 3. Review that list again to see if you have all those qualities you are seeking in someone else. (This is the time for your own personal growth.) 4. Create an open space in your life for this person to come in by freeing yourself from dead-end relationships and casual dates. 5. Be in gratitude to your Higher Power, for your perfect mate is on the way. You won't need to seek your partner out or force the process along. You can watch as events unfold and not be concerned about the outcome. You can relax now.

I was ready to make my list. It included such things as: A spiritual man, a man with a good sense of humor, a man who makes a difference in the world by what he does, a man who is loyal, a man I respect, a man who wants to live on the water, and a man who knows how to take good care of his lady.

As I drove to work each day, I felt grace wash over me as I expressed my gratitude in how Spirit was working in my life. It was an inside-out process of looking at who I was and what I wanted to create in my life. I was able to see my future and rejoice. And instead of just looking for my perfect mate, I began working on myself to become the kind of partner that I wanted in return.

During this time, I was attending a management development class at the hospital where I worked. Eric, our consultant, was teaching us about mission, vision, values, and partnership. I really admired his work. I also admired his cute buns. However, my thoughts did not go any further because at nearly five feet eight inches tall, I envisioned a taller man, perhaps six feet. Eric was coming in at 5 feet 7 inches.

I continued identifying my personal and professional values as I attended Eric's class. Personally, I decided I would never again be in a marriage that had no spiritual foundation or shared values.

I also met with a psychic for the fun of it , and he asked me, "How do you feel about short men?" My response was "Do I have to?" He went on to say that my life partner really knew how to take care of his lady, was highly intelligent, and there was something about a country club. He said our courtship would be easy.

Months later, I hired Eric to do a weekend team-building at the beach for my staff. He offered to drive me there so we could plan the session. During casual conversation, I asked him the location of his office, in a city two hours from me. He told me his office was on Country Club Road.

During that weekend, we noticed each other in a new way. There was attraction there, but neither of us knew what to do with it. He asked if he could drive me home—it was only four hours out of his way!

On the way home, I worked up the courage to tell him I was attracted to him. Fortunately, he felt the same toward me. When Eric walked me to the door, he looked very confused. Later, he told me he hadn't known whether to kiss me or shake my hand. We compromised on a hug. He had a rule that you don't date your clients. But he didn't know that Divine Providence was moving in. He found himself calling my boss the next week to ask permission to date me. After a year's courtship, during which Eric caught up with what I already knew, one hundred friends and our four sons joined us in celebrating our wedding and in blessing our house on the water.

If I had not gone through the process of identifying and living my own values, I could not have asked for them in another person. OK, so I forgot to put "a tall man" on my list. But if I had, I may have missed Eric, my "Find Your Perfect Mate" guy. He may be short in stature, but he's a giant in the way he lives his life and in the way he takes care of his lady.

KAY ALLENBAUGH

"I'm not shooting for a successful relationship at this point. I'm just looking for something that will prevent me from throwing myself in front of a bus. I'm keeping my expectations very, very low. Basically, I'm just looking for a mammal. That's my bottom line, and I'm really very flexible on that, too."

—Lucille, in the movie *Bye Bye Love*

Sleepless in San Francisco

BY AGE THIRTY-FOUR, I WAS LIVING MOST OF MY girlhood dreams. I had a quaint apartment in San Francisco, an interesting job, and great friends. But there was one thing I'd dreamed of that still eluded me—finding someone to love and marry.

I didn't have boyfriends in high school. And in college, it often fell on my roommates to fix me up with blind dates for important weekends. Even in my twenties, long after the asthma, pimples, and fat were gone—when I was actually quite pretty and accomplished—I still didn't see myself as someone another person would want to share a life with. Chalk it up to childhood traumas, big and small. A multitude of things had chipped away at my self-esteem.

Of course, I wasn't aware of the inner beliefs that were keeping true love out of my reach. Now and then someone came along with enough glib charm to put me at ease, and I'd fall head over heels. But these were usually brief romances, brightening my hopes, then dimming them.

Once I launched my career and began working side by side with a lot of fascinating males, I began to really enjoy men as friends. But my love life still consisted mostly of short-term, loose connections with lonely spells in between.

I rarely let myself dream about the big "M" word anymore. This was the commitment-phobic early eighties, when a monogamous relationship that would last through Christmas seemed like too much to ask. Then *Newsweek* came out with the man-shortage article that said a career woman in her thirties had about as much chance of getting married as getting killed by terrorists.

The news was perversely comforting. With simple demographics to blame, I stopped wondering what was wrong with me and started grappling with the idea that I might remain single.

I settled for another tenuous relationship, this time with a man I'd met on vacation in Mexico. Jon was a political aide in San Francisco, a weekend pilot, introspective, good-looking, and fun.

He made it clear that he didn't want me to get serious. Thoughts of a house, kids, and a lawn mower made his skin crawl. Actually, he hoped to be working overseas within a year. It saddens me now to recall how easily I assured him that I had no expectations of a long-term commitment. We continued to see each other off and on, like two planets in orbit, sometimes close but never completely in each other's worlds.

On my birthday, however, Jon was there with lovely gifts of clothes and jewelry, taking me out for dinner and dancing. It seemed to me that we were closer than we'd ever been, and I started to wonder if things might work out after all. Then the next day, he bluntly announced that he was bringing another woman to a party we both planned to attend the following weekend.

I usually cry when I'm angry, but that day my fury was like dry ice as I asked him to leave my apartment. My anger stayed hard and frozen inside me for weeks, even when he called to make amends. He told me that a job had come through—a yearlong assignment in Africa. He wanted things to be right between us before he left, so wouldn't I please have dinner with him?

"No way," I said, surprised that my resolve wasn't melting. "If I let myself feel close to you again, I'll spend another year waiting with hope and doubt and I can't afford to do that. Besides, I expect to be married by the time you get back!" *Married!* Where had *that* come from? Jon couldn't have been more stunned than I was by my proclamation. But he left the country, and while he was gone, miracles happened to me.

Everywhere I went, it seemed I met another attractive man who wanted my phone number. Some of them I met at parties, others came up to me politely on the train, even on the street. These were men who seemed almost old-fashioned in their manners, attentiveness, and regard for me. For the first time in my life, my calendar was crammed with "real dates." One of the men was David, a neighbor in my apartment complex.

An hour into our first date, I felt I'd known David for years. We discovered we shared many hobbies and interests. Before the day was through, we'd already planned our next outing. Soon I was finding flowers at my door and romantic cards in the mail while he was away on business trips. I'd never known a man who was so sweetly persistent, so blatantly smitten, so dependable and generous. Of course I fell in love with him.

Jon returned to San Francisco, bewildered to find me engrossed in wedding plans. I don't know what's happened to him since, but David and I have been married for six happy years.

People used to tell me when I was single that I'd find love when I was "ready." I'd thought I was ready all along, but now I know I wasn't —not until that day on the phone when I loved myself enough to claim what I truly wanted and deserved.

PENELOPE PIETRAS

The Second Time Around

❧

"SUSAN IS A HOPELESS ROMANTIC," I TOLD MY CONGRE-gation. I centered my Sunday talk around Susan and Warren's story. My message was on how love works in mysterious ways. It was a good time to tell this story, because I was renewing my parents' thirty-third-year marriage vows at the end of the service.

At the time Susan entered ministerial school, there was one hard-and-fast rule: If you're married, stay married; if you're divorced, stay divorced. Students were warned this was not the time to be making long-term relationship decisions.

Susan was never one to play by the rules. Partway through her first term of school, she returned home to marry her sweetheart. She brought Warren back with her to school. They seemed the perfect couple.

Susan's friends were shocked when she announced, a short time after her graduation, that she had made a rush decision to get married and it wasn't working out for them. All she could think of was starting her own church and the people she would serve. Susan didn't feel ready to walk that path with Warren. They divorced, and she immersed herself in her new ministerial duties.

Years later, the church was flourishing, yet Susan was searching for a long-term, loving relationship. She bemoaned the reality that most single ministers face—it's awkward to date someone in your congrega-tion, yet difficult to meet anyone "out there." Warren had married someone else after he and Susan parted. She had not seen him for seven years. Susan admitted that in her heart she knew if she had it to do again, she would have stayed with Warren. She realized he had been perfect for her. Now she was looking for someone just like him to marry. Susan felt that if she set her intention on what she really wanted, voiced it, and believed in it, miracles would happen. And so she did.

"I have good news to report," I told my congregation. "Susan and Warren are getting married today." I continued my story, filling in the missing pieces for the congregation. After Warren's second marriage failed, he went through his own spiritual awakening and longed to reconnect with Susan, the love of his life. Warren found Susan's church and tried to work up the nerve to walk in several times. On the third try, he opened the door cautiously and sat in the back row. Susan's heart jumped to her throat when she saw him. She knew intuitively that her prayer had been answered in a most special way. They secretly got reacquainted, and Warren quietly became more active in the church as a volunteer usher.

"I'm a hopeless romantic too," I concluded to my congregation, circling slowly so they could admire my beautiful beaded dress. I could have passed for a bride. I was dressed to the nines to honor my parents and the power of long-term love in their lives. We were all wearing flowers for the upcoming ceremony.

I brought the congregation back to the present and told them that, like Susan, it's been hard for me to date anyone from the church. I even joked that I had heard them all talking behind my back about how John, a new usher, and I would make a great couple. I told them, "Now you know how difficult it is to think of being involved with anyone in the congregation with this kind of gossip!" The congregation roared, and John blushed as bright as the red carnation pinned to his lapel. The service ended, and the ushers moved to the back of the church. I reminded everyone to remain seated so that I could perform the renewal vows for my parents.

I walked to the back of the church and disappeared momentarily around a corner into the lobby. The organist filled the church with the familiar strains of the "Wedding March." The congregation gasped in amazement as I reappeared, walking down the aisle arm in arm with

John. My father walked up to the podium and explained, "There are two ceremonies today. Mine plus Susan and Warren's. Susan and Warren are here today for you to meet. Susan is your minister, Wendy Susan Craig, and Warren is that handsome usher, John Warren Purcell." We walked the length of the center aisle amid laughter, tears of joy, and celebration. Seven years later, I still don't play by the rules.

A visiting minister I had secretly invited to perform the ceremony stood up and met us at the altar. He asked us to repeat after him, and we exchanged our marriage vows to one another—for the second time. "Do you, John, take thee, Wendy . . ." We lit two candles and joined them into one. We kissed tenderly, then placed a banner on the wall behind the altar. As we walked back down the aisle as husband and wife, the congregation read what the banner said: "Love is lovelier the second time around."

REV. WENDY CRAIG-PURCELL

No Signature Required

$\mathcal{JP}$

I'M A PROFESSIONAL HANDWRITING ANALYST. WHILE A great source of financial security, this unique talent wreaked havoc on my love life! Every time I was attracted to a new guy, I immediately analyzed his handwriting in terms of potential for a long and lasting relationship. I didn't want any surprises.

Handwriting analysis proved to be an easy way to eliminate men before I became remotely interested in them. Why bother if we have nothing important in common? Having heard so many stories from my women friends about meeting men who turned out to be "jerks," I felt confident that by using my professional handwriting expertise, I was covering my bases.

On the downside, I kept running out of men to run through my system. After years of hopeful dating and analyzing, I finally admitted to myself that "Mr. Right" probably didn't exist for me.

At a tennis match for singles, I was surprised to meet a man who seemed to have everything I was looking for—sensitivity, intelligence, and financial independence. My intuition told me that this guy looked promising, but I needed to be sure. Aha, I thought. I'll find out what he is really like right away. I'll give him the acid test. I'll have him write something for me and find out the truth.

He adamantly refused! He even laughed. "Why," he asked, "would I do that? You can read things into my handwriting and cut me off before we've really gotten to know each other. No, I want this to be as equal as possible. We can talk, but I'm not going to write for you. At least, not now."

Thus this guy took away my control. By removing the crutch I used to tell me how I felt about a man, he was forcing me to depend on observation, intuition, and feelings. Without my knowledge of graphology, I didn't trust myself, so how was I supposed to trust him?

Handwriting analysis had always enabled me to probe into a man's inner secrets. I could tell whether he forgave easily or held on to grudges. I knew if he was naturally generous or a penny-pincher. I could tell if he was sensitive to the feelings of others or was self-protective and self-absorbed. Many years of study had shown me that first impressions are not always the right ones. I reasoned that if he refused to write for me, it was probably best to forget him. Perhaps he had something to hide! A tug-of-war continued between my heart and my head. "He seems perfect for you," my heart said. "Why not give him a chance?" My ego chimed in at that point: "Be careful. You're on foreign ground."

Handwriting self-analysis had made me painfully aware of my own personality: I was likely never to love again, because of past hurts. A small, quiet voice inside me asked, "Is that the way you want to live the rest of your life?" I knew I had to break with the past, or there would be no future. While my heart and my head battled on, I decided to tough it out. It was time to let go—and trust. I followed my intuition for the first time and continued to see "Mr. Possibly Right."

I now know there are some things in life that I can't control or analyze. When I allowed my heart to open, I learned to be in a relationship fully without knowing the outcome.

I watched this man relate to his children. I respected his sharing and caring ways with his son and daughter. I adored the way his hair curled in the back of his head, the look of love and tenderness in his eyes when he looked at me, the way he never stopped rubbing my thumb with his fingers when we held hands in the movies. At last I knew, with no handwriting to back me up: "Mr. Possibly Right" was "Mr. Right."

And his handwriting, when finally I saw it, merely confirmed what I had already discovered about him by trusting myself.

By design, nothing was in writing as we exchanged our marriage vows. At our wedding ceremony, we simply spoke from our hearts.

IRENE B. LEVITT

ꝰ

"You have forgotten yourself,
and that is your only fault."

—Author unknown

Five-Dollar Psychic

I VOLUNTEERED TO DRIVE OUR CONFERENCE SPEAKER, A professor who spoke on death and dying, to the airport, three hours away. The professor held degrees in sociology and psychology, and he fascinated me with his insights on what made people tick and what was really important in life. I didn't share a lot as we drove, yet he read between the lines. Though I held back, he told me about his personal life and his family. I was surprisingly comfortable with him. It felt as though we had a lot in common. He encouraged me to fulfill my dream of completing my degree in sociology and was making me think about my life in a new way. Out of the blue, he turned to me and said, "You don't have any idea how attractive and charming you are, do you?" He wasn't flirting; he was just observing me. Why didn't I feel attractive? And why had I settled for working for my husband in a job I did not enjoy?

My mind flashed on Allen. My family had warned me against him. "He's not your type," they had all said. At twenty-eight, in a marriage that wasn't exactly sizzling, I was trying hard to convince myself all was well.

A few days later, Jeanne and Darlene commented on how distracted I was at our cooking class. I told my friends I had an unusual feeling of expectancy. They looked at each other and began to speak in unison.

31

I needed to see Reverend Marty, they told me. She is really good at what she does, and she's credible. She's even helped in some investigations with the police and the FBI. Reverend Marty was a psychic.

"Hold on now," I told them. Given my traditional religious beliefs, I could feel myself resisting their advice: "Something is trying to happen for you. You are ripe for a reading!"

I followed them as they drove to Reverend Marty's house. We had decided that I would go first. Resolved to make it tough for Reverend Marty, I wasn't going to say anything—she would have to "know" things on her own.

We pulled up to a small house with a lace curtain on the window. I couldn't believe they had talked me into this. Reluctantly, I followed Jeanne and Darlene to Reverend Marty's front door. A small sign read: REVEREND MARTY, PSYCHIC. READINGS $5.

My cooking pals waited in another room as I stared incredulously at Reverend Marty in her quaint, linoleum-floored kitchen. Reverend Marty was not looking into a crystal ball. Her demeanor surprised me. She was like a grandma—tiny, soft-spoken, and empathic. Reverend Marty came straight to the point by telling me that I had recently met a man from the East Coast who was as comfortable as an old shoe. I was shell-shocked. She described his family perfectly. Again right on target, Reverend Marty said my husband would be taking a trip in a few days. Gently disclosing the heartbreaking news that Allen was being unfaithful, she described several of my friends he had been trying to seduce; and I knew who she meant. I was frozen in my chair. She told me I would have a double loss—my marriage and my job. And I would have a double victory—a new career and a new marriage.

Reverend Marty said I would be happily married to a man who was perfectly suited to me; and we would have a boy and a girl. I was having trouble absorbing all this information. The next voice I heard seemed to be that of my deceased mother-in-law! Although our bond had never been strong, her words sounded tender and wise as she told me to move on with my life without her son. "Honey"—my mother-in-law had always called me that—"he will never change his ways."

Speechless, I felt as if I were in a helicopter, looking down on my life. I saw for the first time that my marriage was a disaster, in which I had felt alone for a long time. I faced what I'd never wanted to see—Allen's repeated pattern of chasing after women and putting me down. My heart ached with the conscious realization.

I was holding back tears when I stepped off Reverend Marty's porch into the night. I spoke briefly to my friends, then rushed to my car. I found the nearest phone booth and called my best friend, Kris. "You'll never believe what I just did," I told her. Kris confirmed my worst fears. "I was approached by Allen," she said gently. "I've struggled a long time whether to tell you this; but I wasn't sure you were ready to hear it. Jan, I'm not the only friend of yours that Allen has approached." She began naming names. It was obvious how much Kris cared for me and how hard it was for her to tell me.

I now knew I wasn't intended to live out my life with Allen. Just hours before, I had been willing to remain stuck in this short-term fraudulent marriage forever because that's what I'd been taught. I was placing a higher value on never divorcing than on the quality of my life. It had taken two encounters—with the professor and with a psychic—to dissolve Allen's hold on me.

When I got home, Allen wasn't there. I scooped up my two dogs, packed a suitcase, and left the house. I never turned back.

One and a half years later, I met and married Jim, the love of my life. I've long since finished school, and Jim finds me irresistible. After twenty years, we're still best friends and lovers. We are blessed with two well-rounded kids, a boy and a girl.

I'm grateful to the professor who unknowingly made a chink in my protective armor. And thank you, Reverend Marty. The five dollars I spent so many years ago was the bargain of a lifetime.

JAN HIBBARD

∽

The Completion

B RUCE AND I HAD A CONVERSATION ONE AFTERNOON about past intimate partners who had been important to each of us. Our intention in being open and honest, sharing our past, was to deepen the intimacy in our own relationship. This level of honesty was refreshing and scary.

I told Bruce about my special relationship with Tom, in my own personal version of *The Bridges of Madison County*. Tom and I had met in the late seventies, when I was assigned to a project thousands of miles from home. We had one of those cosmic attractions. Born on the same day of the same year, we thoroughly enjoyed each other's company. And what passion! Six months later, my project was completed, and I returned home with a heavy heart. Tom and I continued our long-distance romance for the next five years. We spent time together whenever he came to the West Coast in his work as a theatrical producer.

Some time later, Tom relocated to New York, and I went to visit him. Although I loved Tom and enjoyed Manhattan, I couldn't see raising my son in the asphalt jungle, so far away from the quiet forests of Oregon. The relationship seemed to drift. Neither of us was willing to state the obvious. One day we just stopped writing and calling.

From time to time over the next twelve years, I would feel the longing in my heart as I wondered about him. I tried to contact him. New York showed no listing, nor did Washington, D.C., or Los Angeles. I had no idea where Tom could have gone. What had happened to my cosmic love?

At this point in my story, Bruce looked at me with a completely bewildered expression and said, "You mean to tell me that if you were to see this Tom guy today, you might consider being with him again?" Hmm. I really didn't know the answer to that question. But I did know the relationship was unfinished and still occupying a space in my heart. I began to pray and ask for closure—but I had no idea where to find Tom.

Five months later, someone said something that reminded me of Tom, who remained on my mind for the next several days. I renewed my conviction to seek to resolve our relationship. In the middle of that same week, Bruce and I were flying to visit his parents in Montana. We went to the airport, checked in at the counter, and turned to head for the gate. There he was! Tom was standing no more than ten feet away from me. Simultaneously our eyes locked on each other. My heart was beating like crazy. "Tom?" "Alex?" And Bruce gasped, "Tom?"

Our exchange was brief. He had just landed and was changing planes. He was married, had a family, and lived in a large city. His career had followed his passion: the theater. It was midafternoon, and he had the smell of alcohol on his breath. I am in recovery.

As Bruce and I continued on down the corridor to board our flight, I felt a great sense of spaciousness. Bruce looked perplexed. His eyes asked a million questions. I quietly looked at him and said, "Wait, you must understand. God just helped me free an enormous new space for me to be fully in our relationship." I had not truly realized how much space Tom had occupied in my heart.

Seeing Tom and letting him go had renewed my faith in the power of prayer. I had determined *what* to pray for, and like a scene from a superbly crafted play written only for me, God determined *how*.

ALEX MERRIN

ℐ

Black Belt in Dating

※

*S*MILE, TAKE A DEEP BREATH, WALK SLOWLY AND surely . . .

How many times have I had to give myself this pep talk? Ten times? A hundred? Oh, I don't even want to think about it. It's too terrifying for words. The first date. There, I've said it.

You'd think that after twenty years of widowhood I'd get used to the jitters, dry mouth, and mild GI disturbance. You know what I'm talking about—that silly hope and silent prayer that this man will be "the one."

Well, I have learned a few things about dating. I've got bad news and I've got good news. The bad news is it's a numbers game. The good news is . . . it's a numbers game. The secret is persistence, patience, and planning. You've got to suit up and show up. And keep showing up.

I got it down to a science after a while. I always had a "first date" outfit that was appropriate for most situations (usually a brief meeting for coffee or lunch), and I felt I looked fairly decent. I always suggested meeting in the same restaurant. I liked having my own wheels if I suddenly needed to exit. If the waiters ever thought it was odd that I appeared frequently with different men, they never let on. They smiled sympathetically the few times my date decided we would share a main course. Or when, in the case of blind dates, I had to walk across the restaurant to a man who had gained fifty pounds and lost most of his hair since he described himself to me the night before. Smile, take a deep breath, walk slowly and surely . . .

Talk about a numbers game. Some were truly forgettable . . . and yet

I remember them: The tall, gorgeous man who told me the people who killed his wife were out to get him too—as we dined on an outdoor patio facing the street. The usher I had met at church who proceeded to drink seven (yes, seven!) glasses of champagne at brunch and then wanted to drive me to my car. And the pump company president who arrived early for our date. I thought he was the plumber, coming to fix my broken sewer pump. Smile, take a deep breath, walk slowly and surely . . .

Of course, not all first dates were nightmares. There was the world-renowned plastic surgeon who picked me up in a Rolls-Royce and let me drive it around my small town for a week. An oilman who sent his plane to pick me up for a gourmet dinner he cooked for me himself. A policeman who brought ten pounds of carrots and made fresh juice before the date; then checked out my house with gun drawn when we returned after a power failure. The successful restaurant owner who took me to Park City to ski. Smile, take a deep breath, walk slowly and surely . . .

From time to time, I'd get dating burnout and need a "dating fast." During one of my fasts, a no-nonsense counselor helped me surrender many issues that were holding me back from the right relationship. Then my dating became more focused. With that focus came the pain of knowing I'd been picking the wrong men. I needed to look at what kind of man would "wear well" for the rest of my life. Well, for me it wasn't some high-flying businessman. (Oh, darn, you mean he'll have a regular job, not always be working on some big deal?) It wasn't someone who'd been married a couple of times. And I wasn't going to meet him any place I was frequenting. I let everyone know I was open to dating again. Smile, take a deep breath, walk slowly and surely . . .

I don't want to count the nights I wrote in my journal that God must be playing a cruel joke on me. Otherwise why would I have such a longing in my heart for a mate? Year after year, I prayed that either the longing would go away or my soul mate would come into my life. And I kept on dating. Smile, take a deep breath, walk slowly and surely . . .

Now I'm at a crucial moment. I look across the room and see the man who suggested our golden retrievers meet for a walk on our first date. The man who wrote down the names of my friends and relatives, so he'd remember the people who were important to me. The same man who talked about money and sex and fears and hopes and dreams before he even tried to kiss me. The man who contradicted all the preconceived notions I'd ever had about a forty-seven-year-old never-married man.

In this room, I also see our close friends and dear family members. I see our moms crying. I hear Pachelbel's Canon in D playing. I hear my heart beating wildly in my ears. As I begin to cross the room to join him and the pastor, I feel the presence of God, telling me, "Smile, take a deep breath, walk slowly and surely."

CONNIE MERRITT

∽

Soul Mates

CRASH! A GLASS SPILLED OFF MY TRAY ONTO THE FLOOR, breaking and spilling milk all over. My face red, I stooped to pick up some of the glass fragments. "Don't worry, I'll get it," said a male voice. When I looked up, I saw bright blue eyes and a glorious smile looking down upon me. That's how Don and I met—at the University of Colorado campus, summer of 1952. I was there for summer school. Don was in summer school too. He worked busing tables at my sorority dining room.

Don was soon calling me for dates, and I was so smitten that I couldn't eat when in his presence. He was serious and very intelligent, as well as handsome as a prince. I hung on his every word as he showed me Boulder and drove me to the peaks, showing off Colorado's mountainous splendor. I was surprised that he was attracted to me. I felt so young and inadequate. Don treated me like a princess. He treated me as a thinking adult. He was very open, and we could talk feelings—something foreign to me.

That summer was a combination of classes that lasted too long and time with Don that seemed too short. We danced to "I Only Have Eyes for You." And when it came time to return home to Houston, I felt overwhelmed with sadness.

We wrote to each other daily. In September, Don and his brother drove down to Texas to visit me. I was excited and nervous. Scared, actually. The long-distance romance had been like a dream. Now it was reality.

After they left, my dad called me in for a talk. "Trish," he began,

39

"I want you to know that I like your boyfriend. He seems to be a well-mannered, intelligent young man, and I think he will go far in the legal profession. However . . ." And that *however* said it all. "Too many obstacles," my dad said. "Number one, he is Catholic. Number two, he is Italian. And number three, he lives too far away." I was stunned. My heart was in my throat. As if I were far away, I heard Dad talking about Catholics and their lack of birth control, the difference in our backgrounds, and the necessity of my finishing college in Texas. And as though it were all now settled, he finished by saying, "Now I think you had better write that young man and tell him."

In all my eighteen years, I had never crossed my father on anything. It was 1952, and you did what you were told.

My brother had been "the rebel" all our lives, and I had assumed the opposite role. I cried as I wrote that letter, telling Don it was too difficult to continue our relationship. Part of me was scared, anyway. I was in awe that this bright, handsome, outgoing boy could be in love with me. I could not imagine moving away from my family and friends.

I received a nine-page letter back. He told me it was something he had already guessed and how sad he was about it. The letter was tender and understanding, and made gentle efforts to console me. He told me he wanted to leave me with the sweetest and most fragrant memories of the short time we had together. He wanted me to always be able to think back on my summer in Colorado as one of the happiest times of my life.

The letter was so beautiful that I couldn't throw it away. I never did. I kept Don's picture and that letter with my private diaries.

My father died of a heart attack five months later. I wrote to Don to tell him, but I did not hear back.

I began to date and eventually married another man. Someone close to home. Someone who had known Dad and had his approval. Someone who helped carry me through my dad's death. We had four wonderful, beautiful children and many good early years. But we

40

were on different philosophical and spiritual paths, which eventually could no longer be ignored, and after twenty-seven years, our marriage ended.

We sold our house, and I bought a town house. I was putting books on the shelf when I ran across my diary, the picture of Don, and that letter. I unfolded the thin, yellowed pages again and saw tearstains on the letter. I felt compelled to write him—to say hello across the thirty years.

I sat up half the night writing and revising that letter. I told him what had gone on with me. I felt a surge of energy. The words just tumbled onto the page. I told Don that he didn't need to answer that letter, but I needed to write it.

Years earlier, he had told me he would like to practice law in Denver. I looked in a Denver phone book, and there was his name. I sent the letter with excitement and anticipation, assured that somehow I would receive an answer back.

When I saw the familiar handwriting on an envelope a week later, I postponed the moment. I just looked at the letter for some time before opening it. He told me that he had lost his wife three months before, and they had no children. Don had moved to another address after his visit to Houston thirty years before. He had not received my letter telling him about my father's death.

Several months and numerous phone calls later, we decided to meet. We chose a neutral place, Santa Fe. Neither of us had ever been there. When I got off the plane, I looked for Don. I then saw the same smiling face and bright blue eyes, the hair now gray. My heart was in my throat, and my hands shook as we walked toward each other. When we hugged, we bridged thirty years. We immediately fell into a familiar patter of communication, finishing each other's sentences, knowing each other's hearts.

We had a long-distance romance for a year, while I made arrangements to move and he dealt with his loss. We were like soul mates. We married the following April. To my many amazed friends and family who asked, "How can you just pick up and leave family and friends?" my answer was a smile. Inside, to myself, I said, "Watch me."

By this time in my life, I had learned how to know my heart. I had learned how to listen to that small, still voice within, to heed the strong intuitive part of me. I had learned to trust myself.

PATRICIA FORBES GIACOMINI

✍

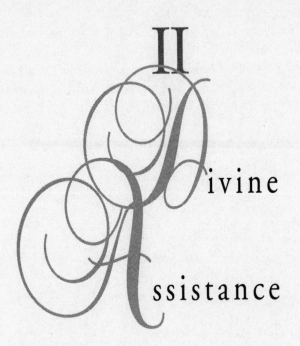

II

Divine Assistance

"*You can let the same force
that makes flowers grow and planets move
run your life, or you can do it yourself.*"

—Marianne Williamson

"I'm convinced that sometimes we have to die a little
before we really live a lot."

—Rosita Perez

Flight #603

ᒍᑭ

I HEARD ALARMING SOUNDS AS THE CONTINENTAL DC-10 took off down the runway. Accelerating to 167 mph, it started its ascent. Suddenly there was an explosion. In terror, I put my head between my knees, and hugged my legs in the crash position. The plane crashed to the ground in flames. In a split second, fire engulfed the entire left side of the aircraft. The flames shot hundreds of feet into the air, and black soot covered everything.

For the previous seven years, I had led the life of a struggling actress in Los Angeles. Emotionally, financially, spiritually, and mentally, I had hit rock bottom. I didn't want to live. As a former Miss Hawaii, I was on my way back to Honolulu to emcee the Miss Hawaii pageant. When I boarded the plane, I said to myself over and over again, "Let my life change; let it never be the same, or let me die." At the moment of the explosion, the focus of my reality shifted dramatically.

From nowhere, an all-encompassing calm descended on me. I felt protected. It was as if a shield surrounded me. I was the center of a white light. Instead of cringing in fear at what was going to happen to the plane and to me, I was suddenly filled with joy and peace. I felt unconditional love.

A white light surrounded me and I heard a message: "You were given

45

this life. What have you done with it?" And then four questions shot through my mind. "Do you love yourself? Do you love your family and friends? Are you living your goals and dreams? And, if you die today, have you left this planet a better place for having been here?" I screamed, "No! I want to live!"

As the flames raged closer, I scrambled to the exit, and I was the last one to make it down my evacuation slide. As I limped away from the burning aircraft, I realized that I had a second chance at life. Anything from now on was a bonus. It was as if all the wrong decisions I'd made in my life were printed on a blackboard, and with an eraser I had wiped them away. With this clean slate, I would be responsible for anything I did from this day forward.

An explosion shattered the aircraft. Survivors ran past me, screaming and crying. Slowly, I limped after them, toward a wire fence. I had walked away from death.

A disaster cuts right to the heart of life. It separates the chaff of pretense from the wheat of truth. It brings out a common denominator of love and compassion for fellow sufferers. A young woman, shaken and crying uncontrollably, clung to the arm of a man who comforted her. An elderly woman sobbed in the arms of a lady friend, who rocked her dearly, as if she were a child. Husbands held their wives as they never had before. Straight from their souls came love, each person giving and receiving in unashamed need.

I now know it's not what you are given in life but what you make of it. Life is a precious gift; and I create my own results.

What am I doing differently? I *never* put off saying "I'm sorry" or "I love you." I look to myself rather than to others for what is happening in my life. I don't know if I'll have a tomorrow, so I live each day as if it were my last.

DONNA HARTLEY

❧

Let Me Know

JP

ESSIE SAT AT THE KITCHEN TABLE, WRITING NOTES. As
I walked through the door, I spotted Reed lying on a pallet beside
Jessie's chair. Reed was Jessie's schnauzer and constant companion for
the past eleven years. They had spent those years joined at the hip.
Now Reed was dying.

Tears springing to my eyes, I slumped in the nearest kitchen chair
and listened as Jessie recalled the memories of bathing Reed while
singing "Sweet Violets." She leaned over and patted his still body and
talked to him in the loving tone of a mother knowing that this would
be the last time he would hear her words. His ears barely twitched in
recognition of the soothing voice he had grown to love over the years.

I couldn't control my grief as I watched my friend go through this
heart-wrenching experience. Finding no words of solace, I bent down,
patted Reed, told him I loved him, and slowly retreated out the door.
I mumbled that I would call later. I drove home, emotionally wrung
out by that sad scene and by the flood of my own painful memories
when my beloved Pepper died.

Hours later, the vet humanely performed the deed we all dread; and
Jessie took Reed home and buried him in the backyard, close to her
flower bed. Such a fitting place for a dog who had been so loyal and
loving. After a brief prayer, Jessie walked into the house and began her
life without Reed.

Later, near bedtime, Jessie went into the kitchen to drink her warm
milk—an evening ritual that had always included small gray paws
fanning the air, begging for an evening treat. Only tonight, and from

now on, there would be no popcorn treat and no Reed. Now there would be only the creaking sounds of an old house that for one person was too big, too lonely, and now too empty.

Drying tears that fell all too easily and too fast, Jessie turned on the evening news for distraction and went to take a shower. As she came out of the bathroom at the end of the hall, she stopped dead in her tracks. There at the top of the stairs was Reed!

"Reed! What are you doing here? You're not supposed to be here!" Jessie cried.

In his usual stiff-legged gait, Reed ran to Jessie, and as she bent down, he eagerly sniffed her face as if nothing had ever happened.

Not knowing what to think, Jessie repeated in an anxious whisper, "Reed, you're not supposed to be here!" Before she could take a breath, Reed was gone.

When Jessie told me what had happened, I automatically asked, "Are you sure it was Reed, Jessie?"

"Yes, I know it was Reed. Just before I carried him out to the car to take him to the vet, I held him to my heart and said, 'I don't know what they do with little fellers like you, so you let me know if you are all right.' Reed was the most obedient dog I've ever had. I told him to let me know—and he did."

SHIRLEY ELKIN

❧

The Sweat Lodge

I COULDN'T BELIEVE I WAS ENTERING A SWEAT LODGE, A place of Native American ritual. I'm blond, blue-eyed, and mostly German. I was forty-three, the mother of four grown boys, and working at a hospital when my husband, Eric, and I took a vacation to the beach with a group of alternative healers.

When we were offered the opportunity of participating in the Indian ceremony, Eric didn't hesitate. He's like that—an "I'll try anything once" kind of guy when it comes to new adventures. Me, I need to be prodded along.

I was still resisting as the twelve of us sat cross-legged in a circle inside the tiny, five-foot-high tentlike structure made up of poles and branches. The Indian medicine woman began chanting and giving praise to the spirits. My heart raced. I watched fearfully as fiery rocks were piled in the center of our circle. Can rocks explode? Will we run out of air? Will I pass out? Everything felt too tight. I tried desperately to control my wild breathing. It was so hot that, in sheer panic, I leaned forward, placing my face in the dirt to cool off.

An hour later, I stumbled out of the lodge. I was totally drained and exhausted. I collapsed outstretched on the sand. Yes. That was it. I was safe and in fresh air. I expected no more. Then suddenly, as I gazed up at the stars, my mother's image appeared before me. I was stunned. (My mother had died young, at forty, when I was just fifteen years old.) Her smiling face took up the space of the full moon.

She began speaking to me in words only I heard. "Look at you!" she said. "You've done so much and come so far. You've had opportunities

49

I never had." She was very pleased with me, and I could feel her love envelop me.

There flashed through my mind all the important events I had not shared with her: my anguish at the time of her death; finding my stoic twin brother outstretched across his bed, sobbing and grieving, six months later; my senior prom, my high school graduation, my college graduation; Mother's Day each year, my wedding day, Mom's grandchildren; a painful divorce, a wonderful second marriage, career changes. I had also wanted to share my spiritual hunger, my tears and laughter, my love of movies, seeing mothers and daughters together. I thought she had missed them all. Now I knew she had been there with me all my life.

She faded away after a few minutes, and I lay there feeling sheer joy and wonder, bathing in the warm afterglow. I can't explain it, yet I know it was real.

If I had chickened out of that sweat lodge, I would have missed one of the most memorable experiences of my life. I was given this sweet opportunity to heal, and to hear Mom say, "I love you, dear daughter."

KAY ALLENBAUGH

What Do You Need?

GOT OFF TO AN EARLY START. BEFORE MY FIRST AP-
pointment, I took a friend to Kansas City International Airport and
drove back by my usual route. Approaching the fork where I would
turn left, I was in the left of four lanes. Then my car began to move
right, almost involuntarily, as if someone had taken the wheel from my
hand and was steering for me.

I spoke to myself out loud, saying, "Why did you do that?" as I
continued to drive along.

My white suit was perfect for this beautiful summer day. Knowing
my tendency to speed in good weather, I put on my cruise control and
enjoyed the scenery. I continued down the highway, singing, when a
voice in my head said, "Slow down." I looked at my speedometer and
saw I was only going sixty mph, so I thought, I'm fine, and waved my
hand dismissively.

A moment later, a voice that sounded as if it came from the back
seat yelled, *"Slow down!"*

Startled, I slammed on my brakes, which brought me to a near stop.
I had just enough time to utter, "What was that all about?" when the
little white car in front of me started losing control.

I immediately moved to the side of the highway, sensing a bad
accident was about to happen. By the time the white car crossed all
three lanes and slammed into the guardrail, going about seventy, I was
at a stop.

The minute I jumped out of my car, another car stopped beside me.
A man rushed over and asked, "Why did you slam on your brakes?

51

Nothing had happened yet." I answered, "I don't know." Then he said, "Thank you. You saved my life!" I asked how, and he went on to say, "I was speeding, going about eighty-five—I'm late and was trying to make up time. I've had so many speeding tickets that when I saw you slam on your brakes, I assumed you saw a cop. So I hit my brakes too. I would have been directly beside that car when it started to lose control."

Still stunned, he got into his car and drove away.

As I approached the wrecked car in the middle of the highway, I whispered to God, "Why me? What do I know about first aid?"

The driver, a pregnant young woman, and her husband were sitting in the white car, both looking badly injured. Blood was everywhere. His teeth were broken, and they were crying and scared. I knew we needed help and an ambulance.

A car stopped, and a woman asked, "What do you need?" I answered, "We need to call the police and an ambulance. These two people are badly injured!" She drove away to find a roadside phone.

As I walked back to the couple to tell them help was on the way, someone yelled from a passing car: "You've got to get them out. There's fluid leaking under the car!"

I went to open the driver's crushed door, when the woman told me it wouldn't budge. There was jagged glass in her window, so I knew she had to exit by the door. Using all my strength, I pulled on it. Unbelievably, the door gave way.

I helped the frightened woman out of her car and set her down, then I ran back for her husband. The passenger door was jammed against the guardrail, and an obstruction blocked the front seat. He could not slide across to get out the driver's side. I shouldered his weight while he hoisted himself up and out the window. I helped him lie down on the road next to his wife.

He was bleeding so badly that I thought to myself: We desperately need two towels. At that moment, a woman stopped her car and yelled, "What do you need?" I told her, and she reached in the back seat for a Kmart bag, which contained two towels she had just purchased. Returning to the couple, I applied a towel tourniquet on the man's arm and placed the other towel under his head.

They were going into shock, and I knew they needed blankets to stay warm. Another woman pulled up and asked, "What do you need?" I said I needed two blankets. She walked to the back of her van, pulled out two blankets from a laundry basket filled with clean bedding, and said she had to leave.

As I covered the man and woman, I realized I had done all I could do on my own. I thought: I need a medic—I need someone right now! I looked up and saw a man in a white uniform on the side of the highway, running toward us. I didn't see any vehicle; he seemed to have appeared out of thin air. He told me he was an off-duty medic. I stepped back as he began to administer first aid to the couple.

I'm sure I looked confused when the police came and told me I could leave. My mind flooded with the grace of the miracle. I had received everything I needed the moment I asked for it. For the first time in my life, I comprehended how safe we really are. Our angels are only a whisper away, to do God's work in our lives.

I realized I had just enough time to get to my appointment. When I arrived, I suddenly remembered, starting through the office door, that I was dressed completely in white. I looked down in disbelief. After all I'd been through, my clothing was spotless.

DIANN ROCHE

"What we are is God's gift to us.
What we become is our gift to God."

—Author unknown

Not Guilty

STRESSED AND TIRED, I WAS DRIVING TO THE MOUN-
tains in southern California. I was a novice, working the twelve-step
program. Even though I had seen miracles in my life, I still struggled
to understand a Higher Power that could and would respond to me
personally.

As I pondered the words of the eleventh step, "We sought through
prayer and meditation to improve our conscious contact with God,"
the word *conscious* kept jumping out. It was at a time when I was
asking, "How does God directly communicate with me by this thing
called 'conscious contact'?" To know, without a doubt, the presence
and power of God was just too much for my intellect to grasp.

At this point in time, there was one thing I knew for certain: The
wreckage of every aspect of my life demonstrated how deeply, pro-
foundly, and irreversibly *guilty* I felt! Shame had permeated my whole
life, from beatings and rape to alcoholism and financial ruin.

So there on the California freeway, cruising toward the refuge of the
mountains, I yelled out to the Creator of the Universe: "OK, I need a

54

sign. Let's have conscious contact! Something concrete! Something now! Let me know that you are real! Reach me. Get a message to me and help me, so there will be no doubt in my mind that you exist." (When you're ignorant, you get away with this approach!)

As I stopped yelling, a silver compact car pulled ahead of me. The personalized California license plate read NT GILTY. I was frozen with the certainty that this was the message my Higher Power wanted me to get. God was sending a message of love and reconciliation, a message that we are not our mistakes, we are not our wounds. We are not our circumstances. We are beloved.

I began to believe I was destined for a life with purpose. I knew I was meant for more than I had experienced in the past.

I attended church the next weekend, and we were invited to stand and state our highest intention for ourselves. I stood and heard myself saying, "I am going to be a minister!" What? Was this true? But truly, I knew. And since I had already received one sign from God, I knew this unexpected intention was simply a more subtle sign, another reminder of how loved I was. I was ready to move beyond myself.

But that's not all. . . .

Years later, a young woman, who had also been sexually abused and battered, was visiting my congregation in Kansas when I shared this story. The next week, as she was eating lunch, she noticed a small silver compact car parking in front of the window where she was sitting. The personalized Kansas license plate read: NT GILTY. The friend who had brought her to my church called me excitedly and said, "Your Sunday message of forgiveness and love has deeply touched my friend's life." I said, Thanks for telling me, and thought to myself, for just a moment: Sure, uh-huh. After years of miracles and thousands of coincidences that had guided me into a fulfilling, purposeful, and joyous life, there was a part of me that still doubted the "invisible helping hands." The hands of the Divine that work constantly to wake us up and guide us.

Driving home from work that night, my doubt was permanently erased. As I joined in the rush-hour traffic inching onto the freeway, a certain silver compact car I've never seen since slipped right in front of me. And like the car in California—you guessed it—the personalized Kansas license plate once again carried God's eternal message to us all: NT GILTY!

REV. MARY OMWAKE

❧

Co-Creating the Future

⚜

IN 1965, I WAS THIRTY-FIVE YEARS OLD AND HAD FIVE young children. My lot in life seemed set—I was a full-time mom. I loved my children very much, but something was definitely missing. As a child and then as a young woman, I had been exposed to a rich and varied education, one that had trained me to question and explore and exercise my intellect. The years trickled by, and I grew increasingly depressed—then I turned to books as a cure. I read voraciously, until I hit upon Abraham H. Maslow's seminal book, *Toward a Psychology of Being,* his study of what makes people joyful, well, and productive— "self-actualizing," he called it. He found that without exception, these people had one thing in common: they valued their work.

I realized I was not neurotic; I was underdeveloped, intellectually and spiritually. Motherhood was not my vocation! I valued and enjoyed family life, but having children was not my "calling." In the mid 1960s, this thought bordered on the radical.

Not long after this epiphany, I was taking a walk in the Connecticut countryside one fateful day in February, still pondering my true purpose in life. The temperature was below zero. I lifted my eyes upward to the heavens, suddenly inspired by the cold but starkly beautiful day, and asked the universe some questions: What's our story? How did we get here? What event in our age is comparable to the birth of Christ? What is happening to our planet? Born of a Jewish agnostic family, I had no religious or metaphysical background whatsoever, but I felt increasingly compelled to explore these broader life issues.

As I reflected on these questions that seemed to have no answers, I

57

felt a message coming back to me, as if I was about to be gifted with a brilliant glimpse of how the world really works. First I saw visions of war, of pollution, of pain. I felt the earth gasping for breath, struggling to carry its load. And then I saw a light in my mind's eye—a planetary light, such as mystics throughout history have seen. I felt that light bathe the earth with love and, in one second, capture everyone's attention. We were one people, we were healed, and we were one with the earth—radiant, alive with joy.

I heard the words *Our story is a birth. What Christ and all the great avatars have come to earth to reveal is happening now. We are one body. We are being born to universal life. Go tell the story, Barbara.*

I was overwhelmed with joy. I had received my vocation!

To me, the meaning of my vision was simple and clear: We are one with God and with nature, and we will not survive as a planet unless we love one another.

My vision has motivated me for more than thirty years. Through lecturing, writing books, and organizing groups, I have talked to people, telling them the story of our birth, teaching them the importance of love and peace. Before I embarked on my journey, I remember telling my still-young children that their mother was a pioneer, that I would never abandon them but I had to go forth and tell the story. My nine-year-old son, Wade, put his arms around me and said, "That's what mothers are for—they are to create the future."

I've never been content to merely observe. Instead, I decided to be an active participant with others in co-creating a loving consciousness for this and future generations.

BARBARA MARX HUBBARD

✐

A Forever Friend

◈

I ENDED UP SITTING NEXT TO JULIE BY CHANCE AT A motivational seminar. We had ample opportunity to tell stories about ourselves and found that we shared a common interest: passion for the spiritual and "unseen" parts of life. I told her I was studying dreamwork. This interest was to become the glue that bound our paths together. At the end of the day, we exchanged business cards and promised to meet again soon.

When we got together for lunch, Julie casually mentioned that she'd been having random and disturbing pains in her lower legs. The next few months proved to be an emotional and pivotal time in Julie's life. She was becoming increasingly immobilized from the pain and from muscle spasms. A litany of physicians, then neurologists, attempted to diagnose her growing lack of control of her extremities. After endless and agonizing tests, Julie had no conclusive answers. She began doing research of her own.

I had never really understood what Lou Gehrig's disease (or ALS) was until it became the focus of Julie's growing suspicions that she was afflicted with this insidious illness. She educated me about the symptoms, treatments, side effects, and, worst of all, prognosis. Unfortunately, her suspicions were confirmed.

Five years after I met Julie, she knew her time was short. We had many conversations concerning her beliefs about death and dying, and how she did not want to be a burden, and how she wanted to pass from this existence with dignity. Julie also had conversations with

God with increasing frequency. Near the end, she heard a voice tell her it was time for her to move from her home into a hospice care facility.

Julie talked often about wanting to leave this earth, and that she was ready to go. This was a difficult, yet special time for me, as I learned to honor the present moment when visiting with her. Time was running out for us. My dear friend was in the active stages of dying. During our last visit together, we made a pact. She said she would contact me, if at all possible, after her death. Due to an out-of-town commitment that could not be postponed, I was not present at Julie's memorial service. A month later, my husband and I went to our beach cabin for the weekend. There, I was able to heal and reflect on this amazingly strong and courageous woman who had taught me so much about the miracle of the human spirit.

On our second night there, I had a very real and intense dream of Julie actually standing in our bedroom. She was radiant, whole, vibrant, and smiling. She held her arms out to me and hugged me hard, and then held me at arms' length so that I could see her eyes and her joy. Julie said clearly, "We do not die!" This was more than a dream—I knew I had experienced something very real. It made sense for Julie to contact me this way. She knew my lifework was based around art and dreams. I shook my husband awake and told him that Julie had visited me, what she said, and how wonderful she looked.

On the way home, I could not stop thinking about the feeling and image of Julie. I began to cry and thought to myself: Julie, your strength and spirit and amazing courage touched many lives and hearts. I, for one, will never be the same for having known you.

Before reaching home, we stopped by our offices to pick up the weekend mail. I found that I had been sent a program from Julie's memorial service. When I opened the envelope, there was Julie's radiant, smiling face on the cover of the leaflet. It was the exact image of her I had seen in my dream! A Native American poem that Julie had selected before her death was printed on the inside page. It began with the words: "Do not stand at my grave and weep, for I am not there," and the last line read: "Do not stand at my grave and weep, for *we do not die.*"

MARLENE L. KING

❧

III

A Woman's Intuition

*"Peace is seeing a sunset
and knowing whom to thank."*

—Author unknown

Letter of Love

❧

THE OCTOBER DAY WAS CRISP AND SUNNY, PERFECT FOR a late-afternoon ride. My daughter, Janice, rode her favorite horse, Lady, and I brought along the dog. We followed the pasture fences, leaves crackling under hooves and feet, and talked about life and love and changes. We talked about how lucky we were to live in such a beautiful place. She told me about the new license plate she had just ordered. SA LA VIE, it would declare. "This is life." It would arrive in January. She had wanted to replace her current plate, PARTY N, with something new, like BLONDIE or SUN FUN. When I expressed surprise at her final choice, she explained that it had come to her at the last minute. I was proud of Janice's poise and grace, the gentle and loving adult she had become. At twenty-two, she was beautiful both inside and out.

Returning home, I felt closer than ever to her. I realized how much a part of each other we are and always have been. When I shared this with my husband and a friend, they suggested that I write Janice a letter, telling her how connected I felt to her. What a wonderful idea, I thought—I'll do it soon. As the holidays came and went, my good intentions faded.

On December 28, at 11:30 P.M., I woke from a fitful sleep. My husband and I were vacationing in Phoenix. I quietly slipped out of the hotel bed and hoped the light from the lamp would not awaken him. I had been thinking of Janice and decided to write that letter of love. My thoughts poured out on the paper, telling her how special our horseback ride had been, how connected I felt to her, and how much I

65

would always love her. Folding the note into an envelope, I relaxed and fell into a peaceful sleep.

At 2:00 A.M., the phone call came that tore our world apart. Janice's heart had failed, the aftermath of a childhood heart murmur. We needed to get home. Our daughter had not survived.

On my way home, I clutched the letter tightly, as if it would somehow keep us connected. As we approached the driveway, a rainbow curved gracefully over the gate: a gift from Janice. I heard her voice in my head, saying, "It's beautiful where I am, Mom." Later that day, the friend who was with her last told me what had happened. They had been driving in his car, and she was laughing when she collapsed and died. He noticed that the dashboard clock had flashed 11:38. It was then that I realized I had been writing the letter during that time. The comfort I felt knowing that at the moment of her transition we were connected through pure love was immeasurable. I knew then that the words I wrote to her were also meant for me. We exist in a new and different relationship now, feeling closer and more a part of each other than ever. And we always will be—connected through pure love.

Her new license plate arrived shortly after her death. SA LA VIE, it read. This is life.

SUSAN MILES

Gifts of the Heart

GIFTS OF THE HEART ARE ESPECIALLY NEEDED DURING the holidays. In this hustle-bustle world, it's so much easier to charge something on a credit card than to give a gift of the heart.

A few years ago, I began to prepare my four children with the notion that that Christmas was going to be a small one. If you have kids like mine, you know the response was "Yeah, sure, Mom, we've heard that before!" I had lost my credibility because I'd told them the same thing the previous year, when I was going through my divorce, but then had gone out and charged every credit card to the max and even invented some creative financing techniques. This year was definitely going to be different, but they weren't buying it.

A week before Christmas, I asked myself, "What do I have that will make this Christmas special?" In all the houses we had lived in before the divorce, I'd made time to be the interior decorator. I learned how to wallpaper, lay ceramic tile, sew curtains out of sheets with matching bedspreads, and more. In this house, there was little time and a lot less money. Plus, I was angry about this ugly rental house, with its red-and-orange carpeting and its turquoise-and-green walls. I refused to put money into it because I had this inner voice that shouted, "We're not going to be here that long!"

Nobody seemed to mind except my daughter Lisa. Though she was only eight years old, I'd always sensed that Lisa was perhaps more family-oriented than any of my other children. The move had been particularly hard on her. She'd lost the security of her old home, and to top it off, had left behind a wonderfully decorated bedroom—papered with daisies—that had been her special haven.

It was time to put my talents to use. I called my ex-husband to discuss gifts for the kids. For Lisa, I asked that he buy a specific bedspread, and I bought the sheets to match.

On Christmas Eve, I spent fifteen dollars on a gallon of paint and also bought the prettiest stationery I'd ever seen. My goal was simple: I'd paint and sew and stay busy till Christmas morning, so I wouldn't have time to feel sorry for myself on such a special family holiday.

That night, I gave each of the children three pieces of stationery with envelopes. At the top of each page were the words: "What I love about my sister Mia," or "What I love about my brother Kris," or "What I love about my sister Lisa," or "What I love about my brother Erik." The kids were fifteen, thirteen, eight, and six, and it took some convincing on my part that they could find even one thing they liked about each other. As they wrote in privacy, I went to my bedroom and wrapped the few store-bought gifts.

When I returned to the kitchen, they had finished their notes and sealed the envelopes, and we exchanged hugs and good-night kisses. The children hurried off to bed, and Lisa was given special permission to sleep in my bed, with the promise not to peek in her room until Christmas morning.

I got started. I finished the curtains, painted the walls, and, in the wee hours of Christmas morn, stepped back to admire my masterpiece. Wait—why not put rainbows and clouds on the walls to match the sheets? So out came my makeup brushes and sponges, and at 5 A.M. I was finished. Too exhausted to think about our poor broken home, I went to my room, where I found Lisa sprawled in my bed. I decided I couldn't sleep with arms and legs all over me, so I gently lifted her up and carried her into her room. As I laid her head on the pillow, she said, "Mommy, is it morning yet?"

"No, sweetie. Keep your eyes closed until Santa comes."

I awoke to Lisa's thank-you. "Wow, Mom, it's beautiful!" We all got up and sat around the tree and opened the few wrapped presents. Then each child was given three envelopes. We read the words with teary eyes and red noses. Then we got to the "baby" of the family, Erik, who, as the youngest, wasn't expecting to be told anything nice. Kris had written: "What I love about my brother Erik is that he's not afraid of anything." Mia wrote: "What I love about my brother Erik is he can talk to anybody." Lisa wrote: "What I love about my brother Erik is he can climb trees higher than anyone!"

Gifts of the heart are what memories are made of. I'm back on my feet financially, and we've since had "big" Christmases, with lots of presents under the tree . . . but when reminiscing about favorite Christmases, we all talk of that one.

I especially remember feeling a gentle tug at my sleeve, a small hand cupped around my ear, and Erik whispering, "Gee, Mom, I didn't even know they liked me!"

SHERYL NICHOLSON

No Simple Solution

ℐℐ

*L*AST WEEK JESSIE WANTED A NEW BARBIE MATTRESS TO replace the one her brother hacked up for his Z-Bots and Mighty Morphin Power Rangers.

This week Jessie wants Ryan, a boy she's just met. "Mom, it was so cool," Jessie says as she chews around her fingernail. I hand her a carrot, which she gnaws with equal resolve. "I'm glad I went to church camp. And this guy Ryan is just so cool. He was in my family group, and we walked around camp, arm in arm, all weekend. He said I was his little sister."

"How old is Ryan?"

"Seventeen. He has this kinky blond hair you can do anything with. He puts in like five hair scrunchies at a time. His ponytail sticks straight up on top of his head, and his hair never gets caught in his earring."

"Hmm. Where does Ryan live?"

"Across the river. He just called and said if I wanted a ride to youth group on Wednesday nights, he'd drive me."

"You don't think this Ryan thing's serious, do you? You just said goodbye to him at camp—what?—a couple of hours ago?"

"Yeah, but you know, he's just being nice, and he wanted to let me know he'll be at youth group this Wednesday, and . . . I was wondering if I could go."

I feel my daughter's childhood slipping away. It's possible. Five years' difference between Jessie and Ryan is nothing. Nothing like the seventeen-year difference between her father and me. It could happen.

"Wednesday service?" I ask. "What about that after-school job you just took on for the Tensfeldts? If you have to leave for youth group at six, when would you do your homework? And track's starting up. A mile or two every day in those brand-new fifty-nine-dollar-on-sale Reeboks is going to eat up a lot of time."

"But Mom, I have to go Wednesday. He still has my blue hair scrunchie."

From Barbie to Ryan, all in one weekend. This isn't supposed to happen until at least eighth grade.

"Wednesday sounds OK." OK for doing homework and jumping on the trampoline and being twelve, *not* fifteen. "Why don't you call and tell him you'll meet him there."

"Really? That is so cool." Jessie dances off with the portable phone.

After showering, I find Jessie sitting against the wall on her bed, surrounded by her collection of stuffed animals. Duke, our greyhound, is sprawled among the colorful heap, with his head in Jessie's lap. "What's up?" I ask as I drop into the swivel rocker next to her bed.

"Mom, a girl answered, and it wasn't Ryan's mother."

"Maybe he has a sister," I offer into the silence.

Jessie rolls her eyes. "Mom, he doesn't have a sister, only little brothers. It was Andrea."

"Who's Andrea?" I feel like I'm trying to read a novel with every other page glued together.

"She was at camp. She's seventeen too, and sometimes I'd see her and Ryan down by the stream, holding hands." I watch the tears form in Jessie's eyes as she chews her pinkie nail down past the quick. I reach for the injured hand, and Jessie lets me hold it as she climbs into my lap. Instead of following my impulse to ask her more questions or put a damper on this whole Ryan thing, I relax and rock her, because there is nothing else to do.

I remember what it was like not to be sure of myself. How important it was to know that someone besides my parents loved me. And how it mattered what everyone but my parents thought. At her age I didn't know what I wanted, but I went after it with a vengeance just the same.

"I just want Ryan and everybody to like me." Jessie strings together the words between ragged breaths and wipes the side of her face against the shoulder of my robe. She lets me rock her and finger the ends of her coarse black hair. I hum a bedtime song we used to sing together, but now I sing alone. I know there is no simple solution.

Love is an inside job.

BURKY ACHILLES

❦

Flower Power

ᏁᏁ

IT IS NOT OUR ENEMIES WHO DO US THE GREATEST harm. Sometimes we permit our uniqueness, individuality, and self-esteem to be eroded little by little, day by day, by those who love us most. I realized that the day I decided why I did not want flowers at my funeral.

I was to speak at a Conference on Human Rights. I went in to kiss our youngest daughter, who was still sleeping, goodbye.

She opened one eye and groaned, "Gross."

I was puzzled. "What's gross?"

"The flowers in your hair, Mom. It's too early for that."

I smiled and headed for the garage. On my way past the kitchen, daughter number two looked up from the morning paper and also communicated with one word: "Tacky."

I stopped smiling. One "gross" and one "tacky" is about all I can take first thing in the morning. As I consulted with the mirror, daughter number three's words haunted me: "How many of the three hundred people there today will have flowers in their hair, Mom? Doesn't that *tell* you something?"

I kept the flowers in my hair. I knew it was not too early. If truth be told, it was almost too late.

Many years later, after having done a session on Creative Living for a board of realtors, I received a card in the mail. It said: "I want you to know that ever since I heard you speak last week, I've been wearing flowers in my hair."

It was signed: "Wayne Cochran, Realtor."

ROSITA PEREZ

ᏁᏁ

Angel on Patrol

JP

*P*OLICE OFFICER BERNIECE JOHNSON WAS WORKING the graveyard shift in downtown Portland, Oregon, one wet, cold night. While cruising, she heard a call go out over the radio about an accident on one of Portland's eight bridges.

Officer Johnson was twenty minutes away from the site of the accident, but she had a strong gut feeling to assist the responding officer. There was no logic to the tug she was feeling. Backup had not been requested, and there were officers closer to the scene than she was. But she proceeded anyway across the Marquam, one of the bridges crossing the Willamette River, separating Portland east from west.

The call was handled quickly, and she started driving back toward the other side of town. Again, she had a strong gut feeling, which held her back from taking the next two bridge entrances. As she was nearing the Fremont Bridge, she heard a voice inside her say, "Turn here."

As Officer Johnson started across the Fremont, she noticed a small car parked illegally off the side of the roadway. The car had its flashing lights on.

Seeing a man and a woman in the parked car, she began her routine check. She peered in the car and asked, "Is there a problem here?"

"Yes," the woman responded, tears streaming down her face. "My husband wants to kill himself by jumping off the bridge."

Procedure calls for the officer to take a suicidal person into custody for an evaluation. Officer Johnson's intuition told her to talk to the despondent man who was sitting behind the steering wheel, staring straight ahead.

She began by giving him reasons why he shouldn't take his life. She told him that nothing was so bad that he needed to take his life over it. Fifteen minutes later, she didn't know what else to say. He looked like he was about to cry. She reassured him by saying, "It takes a strong and sensitive man to be willing to cry. That's how we get our grief out." The man placed his head in his hands, slumped over, and began to weep. Officer Johnson silently prayed, "What do I do now?"

In the back seat, Officer Johnson noticed a baby boy. She told the young father about her own hurt as she grew up with a dad who was emotionally unavailable. The officer reminded him that no matter what he was going through, he could still love and care for his little boy. He could be there to nurture his child, to encourage this small boy as he grows, and to make his son feel safe in the world.

The man cried even harder, and this time Officer Johnson heard God's voice say, "Be quiet!" She prayed silently again: "What do I do now?" It came to her to consciously send this anguished man healing white light. Whether she was moving traffic along, or just standing near the car, shivering, she continued to see him surrounded by white light.

An hour later, like a flower responding to a good watering, the suicidal man rose up from the shower of loving white light being beamed on him by Officer Johnson.

The officer asked the young man to come sit in her patrol car. She had a feeling he wanted to talk with her alone before she let him go. He told her about all the mistakes he'd made in his life. He talked of his problems with his mom and dad. He shared his feelings of despair. His demeanor became soft and peaceful—as if he'd gone through an emotional cleansing.

This once suicidal man turned to the officer and thanked her for being there for him. She touched his arm and whispered gently, "Before you go, I want to tell you something. No matter where you would have gone tonight . . . I would have found you."

KAY ALLENBAUGH

"What you focus on increases."

—Author unknown

The Power of Visualization

WHEN I BEGAN TO WRITE MY BOOK, I DECIDED TO visualize myself signing autographs. Four weeks later, I was invited to attend a Dodger Christmas party given for Los Angeles inner-city children. My date, a former Dodger pitcher, the owner, the manager, and other players would be there to sign autographs for the children.

The children received small baseball helmets when they arrived. The baseball celebrities would sign each of the children's helmets. Lines of small, excited children began to form in front of each player. It was a special Christmas gift for all these young Dodger fans.

A little girl walked over to me and handed me her helmet to sign. I explained to her that I was not a celebrity, but she would not take no for an answer. I decided it would be easier just to sign my name.

Everyone seemed to be looking my way. All kinds of things went through my head. I imagined the players wondering: Who is this woman? I assumed they were thinking: What right does she have to sign her name on a Dodger helmet? What would the parents say when they looked at the helmet and saw all the well-known Dodgers on it, and there would be my name!

Then it hit me. I was actually signing an autograph! This was what I had asked for. I looked up, unprepared for what I saw. In the few seconds it took for me to sign one autograph, a long line of small, beautiful children formed in front of me. Their numbers had multiplied. They were each holding a helmet in their outstretched arms, waiting for my autograph. As I stood there talking with the children, signing autograph after autograph, I was filled with excitement and gratitude. The Christmas party was for the children; but they were giving me a wonderful gift. I now knew the thrill of signing autographs.

Now when I practice the power of visualization, I always see an image of innocent, happy children in the background of my mind. For it is the children who know: anything you dream of can come true.

DANIELLE MARIE

Grandma Knows Best

My mom believed in the most old-fashioned of all principles of etiquette, the written thank-you note.

When my niece, Maura, had her first child, my mother sent a card and a check as a gift to her new great-granddaughter.

The check cleared the bank, so Mom knew someone had received it. But she heard nothing from Maura.

Several months later, I told my mom about Maura's impatient response when I asked her if she'd sent a thank-you card to her grandma: "Aunt Maggie, I sent Grandma a 'cosmic' thank-you."

Mom paused.

"Tell Maura that next time, I'll send her a cosmic check."

MAGGIE BEDROSIAN

Master Plan

I formed a master plan for life
  In the green years' dawning glow,
Not comprehending, naively,
  The truth I could not know.

I only planned for happy hours,
  I sketched in sunny days;
On my horizon not a cloud
  Presaged the storm god's ways.

I left no place, no room at all,
  For grief; could not foresee
That pain and loss were down the way,
  Just waiting there for me.

I could not know my firstborn son
  Would have a stay so brief
And leave behind an emptiness
  Akin to a fallen leaf.

I hadn't left a space for loss,
  I only planned for gain,
But I expected rainbows
  Though unprepared for rain.

My plan was aimed for large success,
  No page contained defeat;
No slow, discouraged footsteps
  Trudged down my private street.

Then when life didn't follow through
  The blueprint I had made,
I couldn't understand at all
  And found myself dismayed.

But life wrote other plans for me,
  Which, wisely, it withheld
Until I learned I needed more
  Than what I'd blithely spelled.

And now in life's gray twilight,
  By pain and sorrow blessed,
I know how wisely life has planned:
  I know its plan was best.

GLADYS LAWLER (AGE 93)

IV

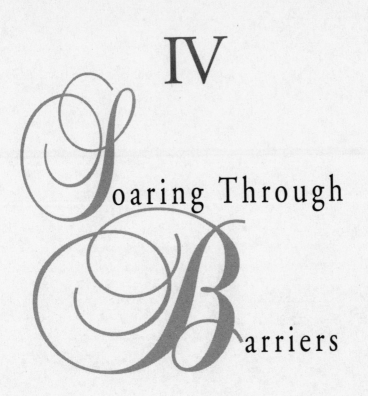

Soaring Through Barriers

৵৵

"When you get into a tight place and everything goes against you, till it seems as though you could not hang on a minute longer, never give up then, for that is just the place and time that the tide will turn."

—Harriet Beecher Stowe

Joe's Picture

MOST OF US ARE AWARE THAT THE FIRST FEW YEARS of school can matter for a lifetime. We know that they are often essential to our success in life and to our self-esteem. Joe's parents were no exception. They saw to it that Joe had a loving and nurturing home life; that his experiences were stimulating and enriching; and that he knew the alphabet and could count to ten. He was indeed ready for first grade.

Joe entered school with great enthusiasm. He liked his classmates and they liked him. He liked his teacher and received encouragement from her and from his parents. All signs pointed to success, and yet success eluded Joe.

He had a hard time grasping the rapid pace of his surroundings. Just as he was on the edge of understanding, the teacher moved to another subject or to another hard lesson. By the end of first grade, he was behind many of his classmates and discouraged. His parents hoped summer would bring growth and maturity and second grade would be better.

But it was not, and by the end of the school year the teacher suggested retention, but Joe's parents said no. At the end of third grade, with Joe falling further behind, the principal suggested that Joe should repeat. Again, his parents said no.

Fourth grade started, and Joe was a nervous wreck. He didn't want to go to school. He had suffered through three years at the bottom of the class, and he certainly did not want to be there again. He had heard that fourth was supposed to be a very hard grade. And it was. He struggled every day and studied every night, but he remained at the bottom—until one black, dreary, rainy afternoon.

Teachers have a sixth sense about the weather. Difficult concepts like fractions call for the sunniest of days. The day began that way, but as the teacher started the lesson, a blackness covered the sky, and the downpour set in. Try as she might to keep them working on their math, thunder and lightning won the battle for their attention. Distracted by the storm, the children were not grasping the math. Except for Joe. He understood. He had all the answers correct. She patted him on the back and told him to go around to the others and explain what he had done. Smiling and happy with his newfound success, Joe moved quickly throughout the room.

As math time ended, the teacher handed each child a sheet of white paper. It was time for art. And all the children did the expected—dark, dreary days always called for dark crayons and dark pictures. And today was no exception. Except for Joe. Joe used bright yellow, orange, and red. A big, bright, glowing sun filled his paper.

Joe started improving and earned his promotion that year. His fourth-grade teacher was curious about the changes in him, and she followed his progress through his high-school years. Why had that one dark and dreary day changed Joe? Who knows what moment a teacher will touch a student?

Joe was not at the top of his class. He did not have to be. He had succeeded and he knew it, and after graduation Joe joined the service and was sent to Vietnam. He did not make it home.

Hearing of Joe's death, the fourth-grade teacher went to his home to pay her respects. Joe's mother welcomed her and told her there was something in Joe's room she wanted to show her. As they entered his room, the mother pointed to Joe's most cherished possession. Hanging on the wall over his bed, neatly matted and framed, was his picture of the big, bright yellow, orange, and red glowing sun. It celebrated the rainy day when he woke up to his own brightness. At the bottom of his picture, in big capital letters, Joe had printed: THIS IS THE DAY I GOT SMART.

PHYLLIS MABRY

Into the Cave

WHAT GETS IN THE WAY OF YOUR DOING ALL THE things you dream of? Could it be fear? It is for me. That's why I signed up for a "Push Through Your Fears and Limiting Beliefs" workshop in California. I was ready to make the effort to push through another layer of fear in my life.

I don't really know what I expected. I pictured sitting around and having meaningful conversations about our fears, praying about them, and that would be it!

So here I am, having just arrived at the lodge, and the first thing they do is load us all on this bus and take us out in the middle of "nowhere" California. Then they tell us that we are going to rappel through a thirty-inch crevass one hundred eighty feet down into a dark cave on our own power! Well now, no one told me *this* was part of the program. Here I am in my nice clothes and gold tennis shoes, jewelry to match, and every hair in place.

Heights are not my thing. All my life I've told myself I get dizzy when I stand on a step stool. I've never broken a bone in my body, nor do I ever intend to. I'd never done anything the least bit physically threatening. I've got to tell you, my "stuff" was really up! It's much easier to *talk* about our fears than to push through them.

This cannot be happening, I remember thinking. "Pure terror" puts it mildly. I was scared to death. Every facade, every pretense, just flew out the window. I was like a babbling, sniveling idiot. I was thinking: How can I get out of this without making a total ass of myself?

They were saying things like, "If you don't do this, you'll have to go home, and you won't get a refund." Well, right away they had my attention!

I knew it was way beyond the money stuff. This jump was really touching a core fear issue for me. Although I knew I had to do this, *I did not want to do it!* They gave us five minutes of instruction. That's it? I felt so inadequate. Like, where's the "real" information that tells me how to do this?

They gave me gloves and harnessed me up in this sling thing. I literally started babbling incoherently to myself. Too afraid to cry, I was feeling crazy . . . victimized . . . angry . . . dumb . . . scared . . . alone. *I had to do this myself!*

I remembered hearing them say, "The next step you take will be the point of no return."

I responded, "Oh my God!"

"Once you step off this ledge, you are absolutely on your own," they cautioned. "If you do not move this rope, you will hang there in space for the rest of your life!"

I'm an Alabama girl. Being in the middle of California with all these strangers, and at least two hundred miles from the nearest Neiman Marcus, I was totally out of my element.

One guy in our group was a career navy officer in air-sea rescue. This man is whistling! I just wanted to slap the snot out of him.

So it was finally my turn, and I *knew* I had to go for it. If you can just imagine the terror I was experiencing and what it took for me to step off that ledge! I had never felt more fear in my *life*—but I stepped off and started going down that rope.

About halfway down, the people who had already descended started yelling up to me, "Look around, it's b-e-a-u-t-i-f-u-l"—and I'm deep in concentration, repeating, "Jesus Christ, Jesus Christ, Jesus Christ." It felt like hours, although it was probably less than thirty minutes as I inched my way down to the cavern floor.

When I finally got to the bottom and they unhooked me, I fell on the ground and kissed the bottom of the cave and said, "Thank you, God," while experiencing an old-fashioned Southern hissy fit—shaking, crying, screaming. The man who worked there, who was un-hooking me, said, "Lady, are you all right?" I said, "Just leave me alone. I'm fine."

I knew then that if someone else had been trapped at the bottom of that cave, I would have done whatever it took to rescue that person. I'd always been there for others. However, standing in that cave, I discovered I could be there for myself. I had faced my fear and rescued the frightened little girl in me.

A wise one once said that true courage is not the absence of fear but learning to act in the presence of fear.

An even wiser one has instructed, "Fear not, little flock. Lo, I am with you always."

REV. EDWENE GAINES

♪

The Perfect Wedding

I'D WAITED A LONG TIME FOR MY WONDERFUL DAVID, and I wanted our wedding to be perfect. To offset my prenuptial jitters, I set out to be the most organized bride in history. Every imaginable detail about the ceremony and reception went into my computer. But there was one thing I couldn't control, and it bothered me a lot.

Mindy, David's teenage daughter back in Chicago, was coming to California for our wedding. In recent months, communication with my soon-to-be stepdaughter had been fraught with both outbursts and silences, as she struggled to come to grips with her dad's new life.

I could empathize with her confusion, but David and I were trying our best to help her feel included in our lives. In those moments when she didn't seem ready to meet us halfway, we wondered if it was even wise to encourage her to attend our wedding. Nevertheless, we sent her a plane ticket and hoped for the best.

On our wedding day, while I was getting dressed, I could hear Mindy and her aunt Jan in the next room, arguing over what Mindy should wear. I knew I should stay out of the fray, but my curiosity got the best of me. Peeking in on their dispute, my heart sank. Mindy was wearing a baggy 1950s vintage housedress, with dark-blue ankle socks and shoes that closely resembled combat boots. "Don't take it personally," I told myself. "Don't let this spoil your day." Still, I was relieved when Jan finally coaxed Mindy into a navy dress with pearls and pumps.

At the church, Mindy stood stoically through the photographs. She said her shoes were hurting her feet, but I knew her discomfort went deeper. I didn't know how else to reach out to her, and a lot of the time

I was too caught up in the flurry of events to mind her moods. But at the hotel, as the band began to play for the first dance, I realized she had disappeared.

"Have you seen her?" I asked David.

"Uh-huh. She asked for the key to our room."

I moaned. I had visions of a toilet-papered room or a short-sheeted bed.

"She wanted to change her clothes." David shrugged.

Just as the band announced that it was time for our families to join us on the dance floor, Mindy reappeared, wearing the baggy dress and combat boots. David took her by the hand and led her around the room in a careful box step. In her self-conscious moves, I saw all of my own awkward adolescence, and in my husband's face, the pride and delight every father feels dancing with his daughter. David obviously didn't care what Mindy was wearing, and at that moment, neither did I. I was happy she was there.

When the reception was over and we went to the bridal suite, the only thing out of place was a piece of hotel stationery, folded on the bed. David opened it and handed it to me with tears in his eyes. "Dear Dad and Penny: Congratulations. I love you both very much. Love, Mindy."

Our wedding was perfect after all.

PENELOPE PIETRAS

❦

"Life is either a daring adventure—or nothing."

—Helen Keller

Close Encounters

ꗊ

MY KAYAKING PARTNER GOT A CALL FROM A RAFTING friend in the Midwest. They'd just gotten a permit to run the highly sought after Selway River in Idaho—a river that could just as easily put you in a body bag as lift your spirits. Forty permits were given out each year to run this river, and we were always among the fourteen thousand people who applied. We'd hit the jackpot. The "put in" date for our six-day wilderness kayak trip was the following Sunday.

My anxiety rose as I remembered the deaths on the Selway three summers before at the same time of year. My kayaking friends had been the unfortunate boaters to be the first on the scene. Graphic details were never spared in kayak war stories, and before I ever met the Selway River, I knew exactly where the boating accident had happened and where the bodies were found.

We met our friends thirty miles from the put in point and discussed the details of the trip. The river was three to four times faster than I had expected a high mountain river to be. My stomach was in knots. I walked to the river's edge and focused on the task at hand. I prayed to God for a safe journey. I had to know in my heart that I was ready and capable to meet the Selway at high water.

I was nervous for good reason. There was five miles of unrelenting Class IV and Class V water—water that foamed, frothed, and curled up into house-size waves and created bus-size keeper holes to eat the unsuspecting. It had rained two days straight, and the river had been rising steadily, along with my anxiety.

My kayaking friends, all men, had tried to quell my jitters by telling me that if I didn't want to run the "juice," I could walk the trail along the river. However, the last time one of them had walked the trail carrying his boat, a rattlesnake had struck the kayak. Choose your death, I thought to myself.

I was edgy, jerky, hyperventilating, and everything that you can't be when you need to muster your focus on reading the water. At one hundred twenty pounds, I float higher on the water than my male counterparts; one of their paddle strokes is equal to two and a half of my strokes.

I pried myself out of the safe little eddy just above the biggest fear of the day—the drop named Ladle. I heard my buddies shout that familiar call, "You gotta want it!"

I'd pulled out too close behind the boater in front of me. This was dangerous for both of us. I wasn't reading the water, I was following another boater, and that's where it started to unravel.

My boat was swept across the foaming water. I was twenty feet to the right of where the safe passage was. Before I knew it, the ledge with the forty-foot-long hole that looked like a keeper from the bank was right underneath me. Time stood still as my boat pitched forward into dead airspace. I began my somersault over the five-foot ledge into the frothing water below. I landed upside down in what felt like a Maytag washing machine. I was being sucked at, pushed up, and pulled down by unexplainable powerful, random forces. My paddle was ripped out of my hand. Miraculously it was stuffed back into my hand by the next torrent. *Yes, you gotta want it.* I righted the kayak with one strong, swift motion.

With that motion, I found myself in the middle of this huge piece of white water, surrounded by total calm. I composed myself, thanked

God, laughed nervously, took two strokes backward, and launched myself into the rest of the drop. Sitting forward, I paddled aggressively, and seconds later, I was united with the other boaters in the eddy below Ladle. The whoops and the cheers made me cry. The pleasure of being alive was overwhelming; I'd survived because of my own skills and the grace of God.

That first night at camp, I again walked to the river's edge, saying my thanks, praying for safety on the river miles ahead.

The rest of the trip was not easy by any stretch, as any of the next drops of white water could have easily kicked my rear. But I paddled into each drop with more certainty than the one before.

Was that my last risky trip? No way. I continue to seek out adventure, over and over. Some may say it was a disaster when I somersaulted into dead airspace and "luckily" paddled myself out of the hole. However, I prefer to think of it as my finest moment.

KIMBERLY JACOBSEN

A Jewel from Mrs. Goldberg

◈

MORE THAN EIGHTEEN THOUSAND MIDDLE EUROPEAN
Jews fled the Hitler regime and found refuge in the city of Shanghai,
China—my parents and I among them.

For years, Shanghai had been the receptacle of human flotsam and
jetsam discarded by the rest of the world for one reason or another. The
arrival of European Jews between 1938 and 1939 was the latest contribu-
tion to the already overcrowded, teeming metropolis on the China coast.

By the time my parents realized they had to leave Germany or perish,
most countries had closed their doors to emigrants. Passage on the few
available ocean liners traveling to the Orient was at a premium, if at all
obtainable.

Miraculous circumstances, strange happenings, and unexplainable
events led my parents to secure passage at the last minute on a German
luxury liner scheduled to sail to China within twelve hours. We had to
be ready. We made it.

Upon arriving in Shanghai, we were greeted by a huge black swastika
riding boldly in the center of the red-and-white flag of the Thousand-
Year Reich as it whipped in the wind high above the harbor from the
roof of the German consulate. Perhaps Adolf Hitler's promise had come
true and his "arm reached wide and far."

The moment we set foot on Chinese soil we were declared stateless
citizens—an awkward position for strangers in a strange land. Like the
rest of the refugees, our little family struggled to survive, and whatever
life my father was able to provide for us came to an abrupt end when
America went to war with Japan.

93

On Pearl Harbor Day, Japanese troops occupied Shanghai. The axis between Germany, Italy, and Japan was formed and once again, Jewish lives were threatened. The Japanese ordered the entire Jewish refugee population to move into a designated area (the worst part of town, already occupied by thousands of locals), allowing little time to find nooks and crannies to call home.

The first thing I learned about being "incarcerated" was that men raged against their confinement and women made curtains. My mother cut up a useless evening gown to make flounces and panels for the one window in the nine-by-twelve cubicle that would house us for the next six years.

We lived on top of each other under the most difficult conditions and learned quickly to make the best of them. Some did better than others, and among those who made a difference in my eleven-year-old life was the round-faced, roly-poly, middle-aged Mrs. Rosa Goldberg.

To find some relief from the steamy-hot, and breathless air of Shanghai's endless summer days, Rosa Goldberg would place her three-legged stool in a shady spot in our garbage-cluttered, stinking lane, seemingly oblivious to its rivers of urine and rows of "honeypots," filled to overflowing with human refuse. Friendly and outgoing, she knew most of the inhabitants of our little "lane" by name. She greeted us each morning with a cheerful smile, a warm twinkle in her deep-brown eyes, and in her "Jewish delicatessen" English accent dispatched us on our way with one bit of wisdom or another. Her message to me never varied.

Each morning as I was on my way to our makeshift warehouse classroom, she would stop me, reach out her hand to grasp mine, pull me to a stop at her side, look up into my face, and ask, "So! What does Mrs. Goldberg tell you every day, little girl?"

Knowing her game well, I shook my head, voiced a quiet I-don't-know, and waited.

"Well, darlink, Mrs. Goldberg will have to tell you again. Now listen and remember what I'm telling you," she instructed. *"Go out and make a miracle today. God's busy, he can't do it all."*

Her face beamed up at me, her hand let go of mine. With a friendly parting pat on my backside, she sent me on my way, giving me a purpose for the day and meaning to my life that will be mine as long as I shall live. She handed me wings to fly, opened my eyes to a world that needed miracles, and gave me the assurance that I could do God's work.

To this moment, every day of my life, each time I leave my house, I hear the raspy, heavy voice of Rosa Goldberg calling to me, and I remember to *go out and make a miracle today. God's busy, he can't do it all.*

URSULA BACON

Mom's Special Day

I N THE EARLY EIGHTIES, WHEN MY TWO SONS WERE toddlers, I put them in day care when I went to work. Like thousands of other working moms, I too was plagued by the articles and news stories about the negative impact of children growing up in day care. Despite the growing ranks of women in the workplace, society's message still seemed to be: "Mothers belong at home with their children." Period! End of discussion.

Although I was doing my best to balance wholesome family life with an aggressive career track, I was filled with guilt and self-doubt. "Am I ruining my kids for life by sending them to day care? Will they resent me? Should I be a stay-at-home mom?"

On Mother's Day 1993, at the traditional eighth-grade Mother's Day tea, the answers to my questions came in a very unexpected way. To celebrate this day, the children had written poems about their mothers. I sat there, listening to poems describing cookie-baking, Halloween-costume-making, birthday-party-giving, and car-pool-driving Moms. There was laughter and plenty of tears as we all heard how our teenage children saw us.

Then it was Justin's turn. As he walked to the front of the room, I held my breath, and my stomach did a flip-flop. How would his poem describe me?

My Mom

How will you be remembered?
Only by the memories you leave behind.
Your memories will be as soft and colorful as a young rose petal.

96

A woman who owned her own business and became very successful,
You will be remembered by the way you fulfilled all your dreams,
How you spent time looking after kids while you reached the top—

Two young boys, rowdy as monkeys.
You were a great mom, a great wife, a great person—
Mom, how on earth did you do it?

Legends will be told about you, Mom.
When I needed help, you were there.
Your shoulder was a place where I could rest my head.

What would I do without you?
How would I survive?
What I'm trying to tell you is, I love you, Mom.

—Justin

In those few glorious moments, as I heard his words, all my doubts and fears about being a working mom were put to rest. Then and there, I knew, after years of baby-sitters, camps, and day care, that my son did not resent me. To the contrary, he let me know that through it all, I was always there when he needed me. He let me know that he was proud of me.

When he finished reading his poem, he looked over at me, sitting in the front row of the audience. He smiled that wide glimmering, silvery smile that only kids with braces are capable of. My first impulse was to race up and wrap my arms around him—like you would a small child—yet I resisted. Justin was a thirteen-year-old young man, and the process of "letting go" had begun. A thumbs-up from one proud mom said it all.

CONNIE HILL

97

Reaching Beyond

Do you reach beyond to touch the sky,
  or lag behind, afraid to try?
Do you reach beyond to learn anew,
  or hesitate—the same old you?
Do you reach beyond to test your limit,
  or do you tell yourself, I'm timid?
Do you reach beyond to lead the pack,
  or do you waste time looking back?
Do you reach beyond and strive to find
  better ways to stretch your mind?
Do you reach beyond to care and share
  and help some others do and dare?
Do you reach beyond, expect the best,
  or have you given up the quest?
Do you reach beyond and claim your space,
  here and now, this time, this place?
Do you reach beyond and try to soar,
  or, sadly, play it safe once more?

SUZY SUTTON

The Courage
to Move On

✥

*"Life shrinks or expands in proportion
to one's courage."*

—Anaïs Nin

Beyond Twin Peaks

I ALWAYS THOUGHT THAT NIGHTMARES HAD ONE THING going for them.

You woke up. Safe.

With the reassuring reality of day, you snuggle deeper into the blankets while your heartbeat slows to normal. This is the way nightmares are *supposed* to progress: first the nightmare, then the relief, and finally the comfortable feeling that the really b-a-d things happen to you only in dreams.

At least that's the way nightmares happened with me until the day I woke up in the recovery room at Duke University Medical Center, to see my husband, George, bending over me. I had asked him to tell me the truth as soon as I opened my eyes. I couldn't bear having to look to see if all of me was still there, if my "twin peaks" were still familiarly in place. To see if I was still "whole." George said, "I love you," and then said, "It was malignant." I remember lying on that bed, flinging my head back and forth on the pillow and screaming, *"No!"* as loudly as the waning anesthesia allowed. And I remember thinking: *This is a nightmare—and I am awake!*

What I had was breast cancer, and it changed my life. Suddenly and completely and forever. I was not safe. Not anymore.

As I lay in my hospital room that day, only dimly aware of the numbing flurry of activity around me, I watched with despair as my lifelong sense of security just floated out the window. Here, in addition to the cancer and the mastectomy, was the nightmare that would never fade: no more security—ever. At first fear colored every aspect of my life, including my language. Even my sentences became jerky and choppy as I grew increasingly anxious.

But then, one day, I thought of my unusual parents. My college professor father and my teacher mother never chose the well-worn paths. Every time I had a problem, faced a crisis, or ran into the various and sundry brick walls that are always a part of growing up, one or the other of them would exclaim: "Isn't that *fascinating!* I wonder how many ways you can deal with this?" And off we would go, exploring possibilities and turning problems into adventures.

Thus, with the terror of a life-threatening, life-altering disease, began the fascination of how to deal with it. Of how to face new challenges. I started hesitantly to confront my new self and the new view that others had of me.

My doctor during this time at Duke was, without question, the most unapproachable man I had ever met. He looked like a Russian czar, massive and dramatic, with a lion's mane of flowing white hair. Everywhere he went, a worshipful, white-coated entourage trotted behind, notebooks in hand, writing down every word he uttered. I would have sworn that even the plants in my room stood straighter when he strode in. He was brusque, all business, always in a hurry. My stomach-turning panic was that this man, in charge of my health—*my life*—scared me to tears. In an abnormal situation, with a desperate need for reassurance and a warm hand on my shaking shoulder, I was totally intimidated by this imposing, off-putting doctor. I began thinking about what I could do to make him think of me as an individual and not a disease, somehow sensing that such a bond would enhance my chances of recovery. *(How fascinating—what are my options?)* I got permission to leave the hospital, went to the mall, and had a T-shirt made for him. A big black T-shirt with big white letters that said: ONE OF AMERICA'S 10 BEST BREAST MEN.

You can only begin to imagine the lump-in-the-throat nervousness with which I presented this silly shirt to Duke's most powerful surgeon. He took one look at it, laughed, and said with quiet astonishment, "You . . . did this . . . for *me?*"

And one more time it hit me: We are all alike. Whatever our role, whatever our profession, whatever our lot in life, all of us are looking for someone to make us feel important. That T-shirt made my brilliant, world-renowned doctor feel important. Imagine that!

The honest facing of reality and the effort to deal with it creatively started affecting other areas of my life. My family relationships became closer and more open. Two weeks after the mastectomy, my ten-year-old son and several of his friends joined me in the kitchen. They looked at me searchingly, and Joe finally blurted out, "Are you wearing your artificial breast today?" "No"—I laughed—"I left it in the bedroom." And off they went outside. My visiting mom asked, "Are you sure you want your sons and friends discussing your breast?" "He's having to face the fact he might lose his mother," I responded. "If he needs to take me to school for show-and-tell to deal with this, I'll be there. Now, there," I said to her, remembering all the times she had said it to me, "is a *fascinating* idea!"

Marvelous things began to happen. I entered upon a speaking career, which has plunged me into the business community and into the fields of medicine, education, charitable institutions, and government. My presentations are not *about* cancer, just *because* of cancer. *(Fascinating! I wonder how many ways there are to deal with each day's celebration of new possibilities, of each day's wonder at what lies ahead.)* Rejoice in your willingness to step out and watch the unfolding.

Having cancer has freed me forever from what I call the Scarlett O'Hara syndrome: "I can make a new friend . . . tomorrow. I can make an impact . . . tomorrow. I can start a new business . . . tomorrow. I can take more risks . . . tomorrow." I've had a smack-in-the-face realization that there may not be three score and ten cards in my deck. Because I am not guaranteed a tomorrow, my life has taken a unique and enriching direction. Today.

Isn't that . . . *fascinating?* I'd always thought that life was about building security. And then a great teacher—cancer—taught me that this is not what life is all about. It taught me that nightmares can become springboards.

How much difference does it make to step outside the bounds of the expected and the ordinary? Five years after finishing the prescribed radiation therapy, I read in the paper that the "doctor from Duke" was coming to Charlotte to do a symposium on breast cancer. As I stepped into the back of the auditorium to hear him speak, he saw me and called out my name: "Emory! Emory Austin!" Five years later, five thousand patients later, he remembered *me*. "My goodness," I thought, "this truly is *fascinating*."

EMORY AUSTIN

꒰

"And the day came when the risk to remain tight in a bud was more painful than the risk it took to blossom."

—Author unknown

Riding the River of Abundance

DURING THE "BATTLE FOR CHILD SUPPORT," I HAD completed my bachelor's, master's, and PhD degrees, while working as a therapist. Although I was very successful in the rest of my life, and happily remarried, I seemed completely inept in the area of getting child support.

My son was twelve, and I had been divorced from his father for eleven years. At one point I triumphed in a court appearance and had the monthly amount raised from $100 to $125. In spite of my efforts, he came through with payments on the average of three months out of twelve.

One day my husband suggested that I fire Chris's father from his apparently reluctant role as provider. When I considered not asking for child support anymore, I uncovered an entrenched set of beliefs:

Women aren't supposed to provide; men are. . . . He means well, give him another chance. . . . He's the only father Chris has. . . . Life is hard work, and you should be grateful for any money that he provides. . . .

As I honestly began to look at my beliefs and feelings, I realized that

I had been angry for years. I was angry at the unfairness of having to grovel for my meager monthly check. I was angry at the beliefs and blinders that had shaped my dependence.

It was very difficult to look at the payoffs for continuing to expect that monthly check. I did not want to let go of the anger. And most difficult, I didn't want to see that my anger had limited Chris's ability to have a relationship with his father. Chris could not form a bond with his step-father, Gay, without resolving his relationship with his father.

I decided to take a leap of faith. Taking a deep breath, I sat down and wrote Chris's father, firing him from any further financial responsibility. Without blame, I added that I was stepping out of the role of mediator in their relationship. Any contact and relationship was up to them.

When I mailed the letter, I felt both exhilarated and blank. Could I really take full responsibility for my financial well-being? The familiarity of feeling like a victim was comfortable; the possibility of creating abundance was not.

I spent many days seeing new possibilities for myself. I needed to jettison the anchor of the past. I realized that I had spent years dragging my bucket to a dry well and complaining about the lack of abundance. When I let go of my small vision of possibility, I began to open to the magical resources of the universe and the rivers and oceans of flow that could carry me toward my deepest dreams.

The next year, my income doubled—along with my self-respect; the year after, it tripled.

With no response from his father, Chris finally closed that door and was adopted by Gay. I watched in gratitude as Chris began to reach out to Gay in both touching and amusing ways—by having rowdy philosophical conversations, or by making fart jokes while playing croquet.

People meeting Gay and Chris for the first time now say, "Chris, you look so much like your father."

KATHLYN HENDRICKS

◈

"Hurdles are in your life for jumping."

—Rev. Sharon Poindexter

Ann's Story

FATE PAID ME A VISIT ON SEPTEMBER 10, 1984, AND MY life—as I had been living it—came to a crashing halt. On that Monday morning, while I was getting ready to go to work, I certainly thought of myself as self-sufficient and independent. I had a job, I drove a car, I had reared a family successfully, I had many interests and friends. My life was full and busy.

Then I fell . . . and couldn't move. . . .

Ever since an automobile accident the year before, I had experienced discomfort in my neck and increasing numbness of my left arm and hand. I found I could relieve the pain and pressure in my neck by dangling my head over the edge of the bed. This is what I was doing on that fateful morning when I slid off the bed and landed on the back of my neck. As my body hit the floor, I felt an excruciating pain—as if my spinal cord had been cut by a knife—followed by a lightning-like sensation surging down my spine and exiting through every nerve ending. Then nothing—no sensation, no movement! I lay crumpled on the floor the way I had fallen and could not move. A horrible realization dawned on me: *I am paralyzed!*

The shock of this discovery was instantaneous. The anguish I felt during those moments was nothing short of despair. "Oh, God, not this!" In less than ten seconds, my life had changed from self-sufficiency to total helplessness. The telephone rang only two feet away from me; and I couldn't move a hand, an arm, or any body part to answer it or to dislodge the receiver. I couldn't summon help. I lay there terrified. Suddenly everything was out of reach and beyond my control. I was fully conscious and painfully aware of my predicament. It was 7:30 A.M. Everyone had left for the day. I was alone. No one was expected to be back before evening. Would I still be alive?

I began to imagine the course this process was likely to take. Given the loss of motor function and sensation I was experiencing, it was probable that my entire body would soon begin to shut down. Breathing would become more and more labored . . . until I lost consciousness. My mind raced on: What if I was comatose when found and couldn't object to being kept alive through mechanical means? The thought of impending death wasn't nearly as frightening as the possibility of having to live totally dependent on the mercy and goodwill of others. Terror engulfed me. An intense rush of self-pity overwhelmed me.

Then something from deep within me stepped forth and took charge, as if to say, "Stop your sniveling! You can't wipe your nose or dry your tears; you will choke. This is not the time to feel sorry for yourself. Use what little time you have left to put your inner house in order." Emotions did not have to run the show. A higher wisdom could prevail. I began to take a good look at my life, now that the end seemed near.

How does one prepare to die—consciously? Not some day when I'm old, but *now,* perhaps in a matter of hours. The thought occurred to me to do a "general confession with an act of contrition," as I had been taught in my Catholic childhood: to ask forgiveness wherever I knew I had wronged someone and to extend mine where I harbored resentment.

After I finished my life review, I felt great relief. I saw my life as having been rich in meaningful experiences; some were very happy, many painful, but it had been an eventful life, with a number of challenges and opportunities for soul growth. I could forgive myself for my shortcomings, which had loomed so large before.

I began to say my goodbyes in my mind. This was truly wrenching. I was so attached to the people I loved. With deep love and caring, I took my leave from those closest to me. I was amazed to see how many people had influenced my life. I began to understand how interconnected we all are. At that moment, it was easy to love the whole world and everybody in it.

Floating on that wave of acceptance and love, my sense was: "It was a good life!" Tranquillity and stillness washed over me. I was at peace. All fear of death had vanished. The sun was high on the horizon now. My breathing was shallow and labored. Death would be a welcome visitor. My last conscious thought was: Into your hands I commend my spirit, O Lord.

The next few weeks were largely shrouded in amnesia. I was told that my coworkers had sent out a "Where is Ann?" alarm when I hadn't come to work that Monday morning. They reached my sister, who also "sensed" that something was wrong. She found me around noon. The first few days I spent in intensive care, my condition critical. Later, I was transferred to a neurological rehabilitation unit.

A major transformation occurred during my six months of immobilization. Often I drifted at will in another dimension of consciousness. I emerged with a new appreciation of life and a renewed sense of purpose. There was something for me to do yet, very different from anything I had done before. Something I could do from a wheelchair if need be.

The next two years were spent convalescing. My medical records state, in part: "Fracture/dislocation of the C5–6 vertebrae with resultant quadriparesis, flaccid paralysis, incomplete spinal cord lesion." What this means is that I couldn't turn a page in a book, brush my teeth, push a button on a telephone, or feed myself. My legs wouldn't carry me. I lived with a catheter.

After months in traction, a spinal fusion, further immobilization in a Halo body jacket, physical rehabilitation, alternative healers, and loving support from kindred spirits, my recovery exceeded the most optimistic medical prognosis. This was verified by a call from an emergency room physician, who said, "I've been going through our records, and I find you've made remarkable progress in your recovery since your accident two years ago. To satisfy my curiosity, would you answer some questions for me? When you were brought to the ER with a traumatic spinal cord injury, all we could do was immobilize you and keep your spine in alignment. The *healing* was up to you. How did you do it?"

I told her of the inner experience, the attitude shift that had occurred in me. Having so little energy, I learned not to waste any. I learned to look for what is central and meaningful. I learned the grace of appreciation. I learned to be still and listen—to live inner-directed. This brush with death was a wake-up call to life.

What does that have to do with getting better physically? Everything! I became more open to new possibilities and receptive to an inflow of goodwill and mercy offered by others. Along with conventional medicine, I also used complementary healing methods, from acupuncture to lovingly made chicken soup. Professionally I retrained so I could counsel those who need a lift in spirit.

Through my work, I now encourage ordinary people to live extraordinary lives. My wheelchair is a thing of the past. I largely forget about my remaining physical challenges, for my life is richer and deeper than I once would have believed possible. What may appear as a setback to many was merely a transformative hurdle God knew I could jump.

ANN V. GRABER

The World Upside Down

♫♫

I HAD JUST TURNED SIXTEEN WHEN MY MOTHER, SISTER, and I were taken into the infamous Auschwitz concentration camp. I watched with despair as my mother was escorted to the gas chambers. At that point, I felt my world turn upside down.

What sustained me during this time warp of horrors were my mother's words. As she was led away, she appealed to my sister and me to live a full life. Her last words to us were, "Remember, they can take *everything* from you *except* what you put in your mind."

I went from feeling victimized by our keepers to the realization that I quite possibly had the inner resources to outlast them. Somehow, with my determination to live, I would overcome their collective decision to eliminate us.

So even as I put on a striped uniform and submitted my hair to the razor, I mentally committed to a return to normalcy, home, and my training classes in gymnastics and dance.

A Nazi officer came to "welcome" the newcomers, and he asked what "talents" we had brought to the camp. My inmates pushed me forward because of my training in ballet. I was forced to dance. With my eyes closed, I envisioned this grotesque prison of horrors as the Budapest Opera House, and I gave the performance of my life. That evening I discovered the power of "doing within when you are without."

Our barracks received some extra rations the next day from the Nazi officer I had danced for—who was none other than Dr. Mengele, Hitler's "Angel of Death," who was known to send people to the "showers" to die if their shoelace was untied.

111

Is it any wonder that when life and death become as casual as flipping a coin, a personality would undergo radical changes? The tenets of "good behavior" learned in my sheltered childhood were replaced by a kind of animal instinct, which instantly smelled out danger and acted to deflect it. During a work detail, my sister was assigned to a brigade that was to leave for another camp. I could not allow us to be separated, and quickly cartwheeled over to her side. I thought I noticed a hint of amusement on the guard's face as he turned the other way, ignoring our clutched hands.

Confronting fear and taking action helped me fight off the numbness that a persistent contact with arbitrary authority can create. Learning to "face the fear and do it anyway" became my way to recapture my self-esteem.

The inhumanity continued, and months later, unconscious from starvation, I was thrown on a heap of corpses and presumed dead. Later that day, the American troops entered the death camp. I was too weak to realize what was happening. A GI looked my way as my hand moved. At the infirmary, he watched over me until I was declared out of danger.

After several months in the hospital, I returned to my hometown of Kassa, on the Hungarian-Czech border. Out of fifteen thousand deportees, seventy of us returned. A neighbor greeted me on the street, saying, "Surprised to see you made it. You were already such a skinny kid when you left."

Several years ago, I traveled back to Auschwitz on those same railroad tracks that took countless thousands to their death. I came to mourn the dead and celebrate the living. I needed to touch the walls, see the bunk beds where we lay those endless nights while the stench of the latrines wafted over us. I needed to relive the dreadful events in as much detail as memory allowed, while feeling the emotional and physical response.

The next step in recovery for me was to go public with my story. Recently, when I asked an audience of three hundred University of

Texas students how many knew what happened at Auschwitz, four hands went up!

I hope that someday my grandchildren will ask me questions about the time when the world was upside down. So that if it starts tilting again, they and millions of others can pour out their collective love and spin the world right side up.

EDITH EVA EGER

❧

Thanks for the Miracle, Sis

❧

M<small>Y</small> D<small>EAR</small> S<small>ISTER</small> S<small>ALLY</small>,

This is a thank-you letter, shared in public because—as you say—it may hold out hope to others.

When I left you in the rehab center in mid-November, a week and a half after your second stroke, at age forty-six, you were paralyzed on your left side, confined to bed, confused about what was happening. Doctors said you could die, or at best subsist with extensive brain damage.

Thank you for proving them wrong.

Oh, the joy of having you and our younger sister, Jill, meet me at the airport in mid-January, just two months later! Precious, upright you—leaning on your cane, your hair freshly cut and styled; tears running down your face. Were your cheeks wetter than mine?

We came to make sure that you would be safe at home alone until your son got home from school and your husband from work. Those few days showed us you would, and taught me far more than I can tell you.

Yes, you still have weakness in your left arm and a slight hearing loss. You mispronounce some words and get confused if we talk too fast, but *you* are intact: your keen intelligence, your delicious sense of humor, your thoughtfulness and generosity, your sweet soul. More folks should be as whole as you are.

And now we see a new side to the shy and sometimes fearful middle sister who preferred to stick close to home, while Jill and I ventured forth and got in trouble. Thank you for your example in courage, fortitude, and the ability to keep putting one foot in front of the other in the face of great odds.

I watched you exercising several times daily to strengthen your left arm: stacking dice and paper cups, moving a dish towel around the table in figure eights, laboriously picking up paper clips and small screws to drop into a cup.

I saw you punch numbers into the automatic teller machine to get your bank balance, then do it all again when you forgot the sum. And I was suddenly ashamed that some days simply getting out of bed seems like too much work for me.

Thank you for the laughter. When you went to have your blood checked weekly to make sure your blood thinner was working, you said you had an appointment at "the vampire's." When you looked at the bleak hospital photos I'd snapped of you attached to snakelike tubes, you said, "I was *really* having a bad hair day!" Boy, are you a lesson in lightening up.

Stopping by your office gave us the opportunity to see how much others care about you (something some folks never discover until a funeral). Your coworkers told me how helpful you'd been when their relatives suffered strokes. They talked about your enthusiasm and generosity when they had babies, or adopted a family at Christmas. Such an outpouring of love!

Several times you apologized for "being trouble." Don't you know how grateful we are, dear Sally, to finally be able to give back to you? Who else but you would present Christmas gifts in January—gifts you'd purchased long before the stroke, now wrapped in paper bags with bows because you couldn't manage gift-wrapping?

Thank you for pointing out what's truly important—and for saying that you've dropped from your list nagging your teenager about his room. "I used to worry about things I thought were problems—like being fat," you said. "Fat isn't a problem. Being healthy is the most important thing in the world." Let me remember that the next time I climb on the scale.

And thanks, too, for the lesson in gentleness with yourself. When you pulled your shirt on inside-out and we called it to your attention, you didn't beat yourself up for making a mistake, as the rest of us do so often when we don't do something perfectly. You simply said, *"Oops, I flunked shirt!"* and fixed it.

I'm the wordsmith, but you say things better. Like when you read through all the nice letters that readers sent when I wrote about your stroke. "People are really nice, aren't they?" you said through tears. And over cocoa, you remarked, "I'm so glad I didn't die. I woulda missed you guys."

We would have missed you, too, Sal. But I want you to know: as painful and as frustrating as this whole experience has been for you and everyone who cares about you, it has been rich in love and lessons. I'm thankful for that.

Because of you, I'll be more patient with the person walking slowly in front of me, or trying to figure out change. Who knows what odds that stranger contends with, that stranger who is some one's father or mother or sister.

And I'm so glad you're mine, my miracle sister. I love you, Sal.

Janny

JANN MITCHELL

It's Never Too Late

ϑᴘ

WITH A FLICK OF A TASSEL, MY LIFELONG DREAM WAS fulfilled. At the age of sixty-eight, I graduated from college—with honors.

It was a triumphant, yet bittersweet, achievement. I had had a loving, happy marriage, filled with travel, friends, and children. Then my husband died. I had never done anything on my own. Ever.

I realized I could sit at home and cry over my loss, or I could do something I had wanted to do all my life. I could go to college.

It was the scariest decision I've ever made.

Even then, making that decision was one thing. Actually doing it was another. I was so nervous my first day of school. I was terrified. Could I find my way around? Would I stick out like a sore thumb? Would the professors think I was a dilettante? Would I be able to do the work? What if everyone was smarter than I?

At the end of the first day, I was so tired.

But I was also elated. I knew I could do it. Although it was hard, the exhilaration of learning new things was worth it. My love of art led me to major in art history. It was a joy to spend my days listening to experts.

One of my unexpected pleasures was being with the other students. The age difference wasn't a problem, although it was a shock at first having kids call me by my first name. They were delightful; we discussed our classes, studied and walked together. One young man even taught me how to use computers. Best of all: no one talked about cholesterol.

I also received a great deal of attention from many of my teachers (most of whom were young enough to be my children). I suppose they weren't used to seeing a student get so excited about their lectures. As time went on, many used me as a resource. In history class, no one else knew what living through the Depression was like. I did, and I was asked to talk about my experiences.

Many of my acquaintances thought I was crazy. Sometimes I thought so too. The papers, exams, the hours of research, the mad dashes to get across campus in time for the next class, the exhaustion. However, it didn't deter me from fulfilling all the academic requirements, including physical education. I was determined to do whatever it took to get my diploma.

My daughters were very supportive. Talk about role reversals. We planned our visits around my school vacation schedule. They helped me with my homework. They commiserated when I talked about a difficult professor and told me to stop worrying so much about getting good grades. (They swore I was getting back at them for all the times they had called me in a panic when they were in school.)

In addition to classroom study, I learned, I could study abroad by taking school-sponsored tours during the summer. One trip took us through Eastern Europe (before the fall of Communism); on another, we explored art in Italy. I had traveled a great deal with my husband, but never by myself. I was apprehensive about going on the first trip alone. However, I met some wonderful people who took me under their wings. I had mastered another step in being on my own.

Little did I know that my college experience would provide knowledge that doesn't come from books. Looking back, I realize that going to school kept me young. I was never bored. I was exposed to new ideas and viewpoints. Most important, I gained confidence, realizing I can accomplish things by myself.

The day before my husband died, he asked me if I would go back to college. He was telling me to go on with my life and fulfill a dream. On my graduation day four years later, I walked across the stage to accept my diploma. I could feel him giving me a standing ovation.

MILDRED COHN

Will You Be Healed?

REBECCA HAD A KIDNEY TRANSPLANT A FEW YEARS ago. Her body went into acute rejection several times, damaging the new kidney so much that this last year it has only been functioning at eight percent.

She'd been losing weight and energy all year. With reservations, Rebecca put her name on the transplant list at a university hospital, but she knew she wasn't totally committed to yet another transplant.

All that she had been through—years of illness and pain, dialysis, surgeries, a rejected transplant—left her depressed and questioning whether or not she wanted to live. A kidney didn't come the first month . . . the second month. It didn't come the third month.

One afternoon, lying in bed alone with her pain and weakness, she realized that she could *choose* to live or die. It was a powerful moment. She was dancing with death. She knew God was near as she relaxed into a deep sense of peace.

Suddenly a jolt of fear and sadness brought her back to the present. She felt regret at the prospect of not fulfilling her dreams. She thought to herself: It's not time yet. I can't let go of my dreams! Dreams of love, a full life, joy, and adventure. At that point, she made a decision. She was choosing life. With a deep resolve, and total commitment, she decided to do whatever it took to be healed.

Miracles began happening. She knew she couldn't go through the emotional and physical healing process alone. She reached out to her best friend, who immediately organized a prayer vigil. Family, friends, and church members prayed for her.

The next day she prayed, "What do I need for healing to happen?" The message she got was that she needed to be with others, to release, surrender, and share her story aloud. But how?

Friends heard her prayer, reached out to her, and bundled her into their car. They drove her to the coast, to an ongoing weekend retreat; its theme was Healing. She silently promised herself she would share her pain on the first night of the retreat, no matter how uncomfortable it felt to her.

Rebecca confided to the group that in the past, she had suffered in silence. On this magical night, however, she opened her heart, and her struggle poured out. Rebecca asked for support. The group listened and shouldered her burden. She found herself going from "Please, God, heal me" to "Yes! Yes! I will be healed."

On Sunday morning, one of the women Rebecca had met during the weekend needed to leave early to drive the two hours back home. Packed, she decided to stay until after the morning meditation. During the meditation, the call came for Rebecca. A new kidney awaited her! She now had a ride ready to go.

Before they left, Rebecca stood in the middle of a healing circle with a group of forty people who sang "Alleluia" as they blessed her, loved her, and sent her healing light for a successful transplant.

Rebecca had the kidney transplant that evening. The next morning, a kidney function test was done. The test results came back high, indicating a need for dialysis. After a dialysis treatment, they tested her again, and the results seemed too good to be true. So they tested a third time, and the even lower rating amazed the medical staff. She was doing better than anyone had imagined was possible. They had not factored in the power of prayer.

Rebecca has a scar on her left side, pointing slightly downward, from the first transplant. Now there is a connecting scar on her right side. They make what she fondly calls "my wonderful smile right in the middle of my belly."

REV. MARY MANIN MORRISSEY

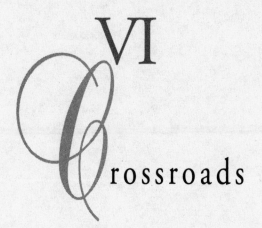

VI

Crossroads

*"Having your way is a lot easier
when you have more than one way."*

—Jennifer James

Better Than a Stocking Stuffer

KIDS DO NOT REALLY BELIEVE THAT THEIR PARENTS will ever die. They don't even like you to get sick. Kids expect Mom to be there always, no matter what.

How well this struck home when I was told I had cancer. I burst out crying when I told my husband, Hank. I worried about how to break the news to our four grown sons. I decided to approach it in the same "blurt it out" fashion we always used in our family . . . so when the first one called on the phone:

"Hi, Mom."

"Hi, babe."

"How are you?"

"Not too good. I just got bad news. The doctor says I have cancer."

Long pause . . . and then the kid says, "Does that mean you're going to die?"

The second one calls:

"Hi, Mom."

"Hi, babe."

"What's up?"

"Nothing good, I'm afraid. I've just been told I have breast cancer."

Long pause . . . and then the kid says, "But, Mom . . . you don't even eat fat."

The third one calls:

"Hi, Mom."

"Hi, babe."

"How's life treating you?"

"Not well. I just found out I have breast cancer."

Long pause . . . and then the kid says, "This isn't going to bother Dad, is it?"

The fourth one calls:

"Hi, Mom."

"Hi, babe."

"What's new?"

"Nothing good. The doctor says I have cancer."

Long pause . . . and then the kid says, "Why couldn't it have been Mrs. Walcott?" (Mrs. Walcott was a neighbor who loved chasing the kids off her sidewalk, screaming and waving a broom.)

Well, that all took place on December 4, 1987. On Saturday, December 5, two days before the removal of my breast, I went in for a chest X ray and a bone scan. I had announced to my family that if the cancer had spread through my body, I was not having the surgery. Hank wanted to go with me for the tests. I said, "No, I can only handle my own emotions this time. I don't need a husband pacing back and forth in the waiting room. It would be just our luck to be billed for a hole in the carpet."

I spent the whole day taking my clothes off and putting them on again. Each test was conducted inside a cold cubicle. With each test, the nurses would glide in on squeakless shoes to take blood from my arm or X-ray my chest. Then, as quickly and as quietly, they would leave me with my terror, without even a trace of perfume to mark their exit.

Men in white coats marched in, with their cold hands and vacant smiles. They poked and prodded, while I sat in quiet terror, waiting for the doctor to deliver the final crushing blow, telling me that the cancer had spread. I was terrified as I waited.

Suddenly the doctor appeared. He said, "I see no other cancer in the rest of your body." Oh, how I prayed this man had twenty-twenty vision.

I drove home as if by magic. I skidded into our driveway, jumped out of the car, and ran toward our front door. And then I heard music

126

bellowing out from our living room. It was Mahalia Jackson, singing "Silent Night." I threw open the door and stepped inside. In the corner of the living room stood the largest Christmas tree we had ever had, decorated with all the ornaments the kids had ever made . . . even the ugly ones. Standing there was my family, each one dressed in a suit and tie. They looked as if they were ready to carry me down the aisle in a box.

"Merry Christmas, Mom," they shouted.

"Merry Christmas," I whispered, "and a Happy New Year . . . I know we have lots more to come." We hugged each other as we sobbed. And then I saw the dining room table set with the good china, the good silver, and all the chipped crystal.

That night together was one of the best we've ever had. My family never looked so precious . . . and Domino's Pizza never tasted so good.

LOLA D. GILLEBAARD

ℐℐ

"For something new to begin, something must end."

—Kris King

The Interview

As a young woman in the early seventies, I worked at a job in a small southern Louisiana town, doing door-to-door interviews. I was collecting political-sociological research data for a PhD candidate. I had a letter of introduction from the mayor and the chief of police, to put residents at ease.

I will never forget one man whom I interviewed. He was the owner of a major business in town and highly respected by the community. He invited me into his home for the twenty-minute interview. It was a hot, humid summer day.

One part of the interview involved rating groups of people on a scale of one to ten. There were twenty categories, including business people and farmers, men and women, Republicans and Democrats. He was answering right along, until I asked him about Catholics and Protestants.

He stopped. He asked me what religion I practiced. I explained that it was best not to tell him, so as not to bias his responses. Apparently not wishing to offend me, he rated both religious groups equally high.

The next category was Jews. Not knowing that I was Jewish, he began to tell me that he knew all about "those people," because he had served with them in the army. "You know," he told me, "there's probably a prince or two among them, but other than that, every last one of them are dirty and evil-spirited."

I began to feel frightened. I was a young Jewish woman alone in a house with a man who was not only anti-Semitic but self-righteous about his bigotry. All I wanted to do was finish the interview and get out of the house and as far away from him as I could.

He continued ranting about Jews and, at the same time, asking me if I was Catholic or Protestant. I continued to smile and explain why it was best I not answer. He went on, "You know them Jews. They're dirty and they stink. They'll go days and days without even changing their socks or underwear. And talk about greed. Why, they'll rob you of your last drop of blood if it'll get them a dime."

My fear rising, I finished the interview and said goodbye. When I got outside, he asked me one more time about my religion. I wanted to run away from his house, from his hatred. But I couldn't bring myself to leave him with his arrogant, "knowing" prejudice. So, feeling some safety with the screen door between us, I told him the truth. "Sir," I said, "I am Jewish."

He looked at me for a second and then said, "Well, I told you there was a prince or two among them. I must have just met one."

"No, sir," I replied, "you have met a human being who happens to be Jewish. No prince, not even a princess. A human being just like you."

His smile disappeared, and my fear came back. But after what seemed like eternity, with the two of us staring at one another, his voice got soft and his head bowed. "Ma'am," he said, "I'm sorry."

SHELLY MARKS

And I Almost Didn't Go

WHAT ARE YOU GOING TO WEAR?" MY HUSBAND HAD that innocent look on his face that typically masked his emotions. But after fifteen years of marriage, I knew what he was really wondering: Is it appropriate?

Not that I dress inappropriately. In fact, I "gussy up" real fine, thank you. But David was nervous. After all, it isn't often that you invite legendary pianist Van Cliburn to dinner.

"Look . . ." I was spoiling for a fight. "If you'd rather I stay home, I'd be glad to. You waited so long to get a sitter that I sorta think you don't want me, anyway."

The second salvo was launched. The tension in our home had been growing ever since David called Cliburn's personal manager. He invited Van first to dinner with VIPs from the Saint Louis music community, and then to appear the next day to sign Steinways at our piano store. Needless to say, David was tightly strung. Cliburn is a national treasure, an immortal in the music world; and we had moved to Saint Louis to start this business only two years before. If the dinner and appearance went well, it would be the climax of the great start our piano gallery had enjoyed here. If it went poorly, the repair work could be extensive.

I also had reason to feel panic. As David once said, "People seem to either love you or hate you." There seemed to be no middle road, no lukewarm feelings, when it came to *moi*.

Then, too, my knowledge of music was rather limited. True, my mother had been a professional ballerina. I had grown up hearing the classics. But when it came to naming what I heard, or recalling who conducted the Chicago Symphony, or even telling the difference between Bach and Beethoven, I was lost. As I dressed for the dinner, I gnashed my teeth and muttered, "I will be charming. I will be charming. I will be charming."

I had visions of a very short, very embarrassing, stab at conversation: *So, Mr. Cliburn, your piano has eighty-eight keys . . . ?*

At the restaurant, our dinner party was so large that we had to be split into two tables. David told me I would sit next to Mr. Cliburn.

"Call me Van," said the long, tall Texan who had taken Russia by storm.

He chatted gracefully with everyone at the table. Mainly they discussed conductors and symphony halls around the world. I excused myself to check on Franz, one of my friends at the other table. He was eating a large, succulent Portobello mushroom. I helped myself to a bite.

When I returned to my seat, I explained my absence.

"Sorry. I just can't seem to resist food on other people's plates."

Van looked at me curiously. "Neither can I. I'm afraid I'm positively shameless."

And so began a friendship born, if not in heaven, at least at Tony's, a five-star restaurant, an earthly version of paradise for those of us who love food. Van sipped my tomato soup. I ate one of his scallops. Back and forth we went all evening, eating and discussing . . . performing. You see, I'm a speaker, and his thoughts on audiences, practice, and nerves were music to my ears.

We munched and sipped our way through the courses and sealed our friendship with—what else?—dessert. He insisted I taste a frothy Italian delicacy, and I enticed him into spoonfuls of an ice cream pie smothered in caramel sauce. Finally, I pushed the plate away.

Van looked at it lustfully. "You aren't going to finish that?"

I giggled. "No, but you are!" and I slid my plate over in front of him.

Well, I suppose that strictly speaking, one dinner does not a friendship make. But I don't know, maybe it does when you meet a kindred spirit over chow. Someone who likes the same food and worries the same worries you do is hard to find.

And to think I almost didn't go.

JOANNA SLAN

ℐℐ

Stranded at the Truck Stop

ↀↀ

I WAS DRIVING HOME TO TAHOE CITY FROM SAN Francisco after a speaking engagement. Weather reports predicted a major snowstorm on the pass, and I was hoping to be ahead of it. As I pulled into Auburn, California, I was surprised to see that the highway patrol had blocked the roads due to "whiteout" blizzard conditions. No one was getting through the barricades. Well, this was a new one for me. I went to the first, second, and third motels in Auburn, and there was no room at the inn! Finally, I found space at the fourth motel—a truck stop.

I checked in, turned to leave the lobby, and bumped into a fabulous-looking gentleman. He introduced himself as Dennis.

"Since we're stranded," he said, "how about we have dinner to-gether?" I quickly gave him the once-over and felt safe.

"Sure," I said. "Let me just go up to my room and unpack, and I'll meet you in the restaurant across the street."

I was so relieved to have a room, I didn't even mind the paper-thin walls of this low-budget motel. I was happy just to have a roof over my head!

I heard a man's voice next door. He's talking on the phone. In this deep, husky voice, I hear, "Yeah, I'm on overtime. I'm stranded in Auburn and had to park my rig. Don't get me wrong, though, all's not lost. I just met this redhead in the lobby. I'm going to take her out to dinner, give her some liquor, and look out later!"

I couldn't believe I was hearing this. It was Dennis! Then I realized I was in one of those suites with connecting doors.

I knocked on his adjoining door.

"Dennis, can you do me a favor?" I asked.

"Where are you?" he questioned.

"Right here," I responded. "We have connecting rooms."

He opened his door and said, "Sure, you need something? Just name it."

"Well, listen," I told him. "When you bring that redhead back from dinner, will you promise to keep it down. I can hear everything through these walls."

I missed dinner that night; and by morning I was starving. Knowing there was safety in numbers, I went to breakfast in the coffee shop—with twenty-five truckers.

I peered out the window, and there was Dennis. He was getting into his truck. No wonder I suspected something was up after hearing that phone call the night before. The sign on the side read: FRITO LAY.

DONNA HARTLEY

High-Tech Wisdom

ᏔᎶ

MOM, GO OUT OF YOUR ROOM AND DON'T PEEK. I'VE got a surprise for you. You're going to love it."

I waited joyfully in another part of my tiny house. My adult kids always know what kind of toys I like, and I imagined a new meditation candle, a Native American ceremonial object, a plant—probably something spiritual. Several minutes passed, and my curiosity grew.

"It isn't totally ready, but you can come in now." Carol's eyes were dancing in anticipation of my reaction. I immediately spotted the monstrosity sitting on top of my formerly uncluttered desk, taking up most of the space.

"Isn't it great, Mom! My school is involved in a special project, and all the teachers get the latest-model computers. I want you to have my old model. It's perfect for you. I'll even give you personal instructions."

I longed to give my daughter the enthusiastic reaction she expected, but she would see through my lies. The aversion was all over my face, and the truth spilled out of my mouth. "Honey, thank you, but I don't do computers. I'm from the dinosaur age of manual typewriters and carbon paper. My first television was black and white, and my first 'plane ride' was on a train."

"Mom, I know you can learn this, and you'll love it. I even brought you a mouse." I was hoping she meant a rodent, but I knew she was referring to that ugly object with a tangled gray cord for a tail.

The computer sat there, a silent reminder of my incompetence and unwillingness to enter the electronic age. I was always considered to be

135

"with-it" by my kids and their friends, but now my reputation was tarnished.

Months passed. My typewriter met my needs just fine, even though I was on a constant drug high from white-out fumes. That obsolete friend must have known its days were numbered when it broke down and died. I couldn't find a typewriter repair store that was still in business. I knew that the time had come to enter the world of Macs, modems, and mice.

"Carol, I'm ready to learn to be a computer whiz. Help!" She came immediately, triumph oozing from every pore. She was ready to take on her most challenging pupil. I sort of understood what she was explaining, and by the end of the day, I could work the on and off switch. The truth is I took to the computer like peanut butter takes to jelly and within weeks was an addict, spending hours writing to everyone. Actually, that is an exaggeration; the hours were spent playing computer solitaire. I spent more time with my mouse than my spouse.

It is such a thrill to open my mind to the new computer age—using the delete key on my "I can't do it" killer self-talk. My next milestone will be to go on-line and float around in cyberspace.

I'm glad the computer takes up so much room. There are moments in my life when I need a big reminder that opportunities for growth are always there.

LYNNE GOLDKLANG

Little Glass Angel

ℒISA HOPPED INTO THE BACK SEAT OF THE CAR, BUB-
bling over with excitement. She'd found the *perfect* Christmas gift for
every member of our family.

As we pulled away from the curb, Lisa whispered to me, "Oh,
Mama, I got Daddy a shirt for fifteen dollars, I bought Joey a race car
for ten dollars, and I bought Rags a bag of bones to chew on for six
ninety-five. And Mama, I think you're gonna *love* what I bought you."

I knew how much money Lisa had taken to the mall. Now I knew
what she'd spent for Christmas gifts. Quickly adding up what she'd
spent on her dad, her brother, and the dog, I became clearly aware that
what she'd spent on the dog was more than she'd spent on me.

I felt a slow, growing sickness in the pit of my stomach. *Lisa, how
could you spend more money on the dog than you did on me? I've loved
you, cared for you, would gladly give my life for you! How could you think
so little of me?* The unspoken turned from hurt to anger. She and her
brother chattered away. I said nothing, resentment growing inside.

We arrived home and got out of the car in silence. The kids followed
me inside. Lisa was still giddy with excitement over Christmas, and she
was proud of her gifts. She asked if I'd like to see the presents she'd
bought the others.

"No," I snapped. "I don't want to see anything."

"Mama, what's wrong?"

"Nothing." My lie was obvious.

"Mama, I know something's wrong. What is it?"

I could hardly stand myself. I was nearly forty years old and churning inside because my daughter had spent more money on the dog than on me. I couldn't believe my own immaturity, but I couldn't seem to do anything about my feelings.

"Lisa, I'm acting like a child right now because you spent more for the dog's Christmas present than you did on me. I wish I didn't feel like this, but I do. I'm going upstairs, and when I feel like acting like an adult, I'll be back down. In the meantime, that's how I feel."

"Mama," she shrieked incredulously, "I didn't even think about how much it cost. I found your gift *first,* and I bought it because I knew you would love it." She then burst into tears. "Now I don't feel like giving anybody anything. I wish I hadn't even gone shopping."

I felt horrible . . . but the feelings kept coming. I bolted to my bedroom, fell on the bed, and sobbed. After the tears were gone, I lay in the darkness thinking: *How could I have behaved so badly with Lisa, whom I dearly love?* Perhaps It was because I didn't feel loved. But I knew she loved me. I washed my face, slipped downstairs, apologized to my daughter, and asked her forgiveness. Although I could never take back the hurt I had caused her, it was the best I could do.

I shared this story years later with a friend, who said, "Don't you see, Mary Jane? She didn't need to buy your love; she already had it."

I did not love myself enough at that time to see the beauty of her inexpensive gift. Lisa's glass angel was a gift of love. Love has no price tag.

That happened years ago. Yet every Christmas when I gingerly unfold the tissue that holds my little glass angel with the Wedgwood-blue candle, I am reminded of the greatest gift of all . . . and of the priceless child who gave it.

MARY JANE MAPES

✐

Cool Blades on the Boardwalk

JP

IT WAS A VAGUE FAMILIAR FEELING—A FEELING OF freedom experienced a lifetime ago. Motion. Speed. Wind. Excitement. Small but present danger. Oh, yes! That same exhilaration that comes with competence. I was doing it!

I was rollerblading on the boardwalk at Seaside, Oregon, on a glorious late-summer afternoon. Two miles of flat, smooth pavement, sunshine, ocean air. I couldn't help but smile; it was as ridiculously relentless as a yellow happy face. My body moved with relative ease and a modicum of grace. Push, glide, push, glide . . . don't lift the feet so high. Swing the hips. *Oops!* Too much push means too much glide. Let's get more control here. Up and down! Up and down! Miles and miles . . . every once in a while picking up the scent of a cigar, as I once again whizzed past my husband, reading Tom Clancy on a bench.

Getting tired, I informed my husband that on the next pass I wanted to stop. "OK," he said. "I'll be ready." Stopping is not yet a skill I have mastered. As I approached him, I slowed to a more manageable speed. He stood up, swung his arms wide, and enfolded me in a great hug. "I am your stopping place," he whispered. And I thought: Yes. What a wonderful metaphor. You are my safe, comfortable stopping post.

I sat for a while on the bench, enjoying that moment in my life. Some teenagers sauntered past, talking quietly among themselves. The last, a young man about thirteen, looked admiringly at my skates, bent down, and murmured just so we could hear, "Cool blades." Then he picked up his pace to catch his friends. My husband and I said in unison, "Cool blades!?" And we laughed.

The sunset watchers began converging like 49er fans on Super Bowl Sunday. I hoisted myself off the bench to make the most of the fading sunlight with another run. Up and down, push and glide. Lost in the exquisite rhythm and the elegant air, I almost missed the group of women. But out of the corner of my eye, I glimpsed a bicycle surrey pulled up close to the boardwalk. Four women nested there comfortably, in that distinctly women's way of companionable silence. I thought they were completely absorbed in the inch-by-inch disappearance of the day. But as I moved past, almost out of earshot, I heard the soft call of support, "Go, girl!" To acknowledge, I signaled with a "thumbs up" and continued on.

Now, whenever I put on my skates, I hear the voice saying, "Cool blades," and I smile. When I think of my husband as a safe stopping place, I smile. When I replay the sisterly words of support, I smile. I'm sure glad I didn't take seriously those people who predicted, "Rollerblade? You're nearly sixty! You'll kill yourself!"

Kill myself? I'd say I was very much alive and well on the boardwalk!

PAM GROSS

❦

VII

Going the Distance

"*I'm not afraid of storms,
for I am learning how to sail my ship.*"

—Louisa May Alcott

Raggedy Ann and Me

ONE DAY, WHEN I WAS SIX AND MY SISTER WAS EIGHT, my mother brought home a beautiful handmade Raggedy Ann and Raggedy Andy. Mother had us whisper in her ear which one we wanted. Of course, I wanted the little girl with the red heart that said "I love you." Yet, when it was my turn, knowing my sister wanted Raggedy Ann, I murmured, "Raggedy Andy." For years, I pretended to myself and others that I loved my Raggedy Andy.

I had plenty of reasons for choosing Raggedy Andy. Aware it would be too hard on Mother if my sister and I chose the same doll, I took care of Mother. Also, I feared my sister's anger and envy if I won. I didn't feel brave enough to have something for myself at her expense! For all these reasons, it just wasn't safe. The way I resolved my dilemma was to accommodate and not want at all.

It's significant that I couldn't let myself choose the doll I wanted, but even more crucial was my inability to let *myself* know for more than a moment that I wanted her. I not only fooled them, I fooled myself!

Later, in the course of therapy as a young woman, I told my husband the story of how I didn't choose Raggedy Ann. I was astonished to find myself weeping, releasing tears that had been locked up for twenty years. I wept for the loss of Raggedy Ann, and even more for the loss of the little girl who had to give up herself to keep peace in her family. Not being able to be who I was and want what I wanted was a source of great suffering for me.

On my next birthday, my husband watched as I opened his gift. The box was sealed with children's wrapping paper. I tore the paper off the box and lifted the lid. There she was peeking out of the tissue—my very own Raggedy Ann.

I now have a small collection of Raggedy Ann dolls. She has become a symbol to me of my reclaimed self. My newest Raggedy Ann is three feet tall and graces a small rocker in my bedroom. She happily reminds me that it's OK to know what I want, and it's OK to give to myself. It's now safe to be me.

CHRISTINE B. EVANS

❧

"Love is an endless act of forgiveness."

—Author unknown

A Legacy of Love

FROM TIME TO TIME, AN EXPERIENCE OF ASTONISHING grace can instantaneously transform our relationship to self, others, and the universe in a way that leaves us renewed. The story of my mother's death and our mutual rebirth was that kind of luminous event.

My mother's answer to the perennial question of why bad things happen to good people was deeply affected by her losing most of her family in the Holocaust. Her faith was shattered by Hitler. To her, the world was a Godless place where nice guys finished last. After my father fell ill with leukemia and committed suicide when medical treatments had rendered his life unbearable, my mother became a hermit. She saw only family for the last thirteen years of her life.

When my mother's health failed and she became bedridden, I wondered how she felt about death. After all, my entire professional life consisted of working with people in passages like my mother's. But with her, I felt stymied. It was a case of the shoemaker's children having no shoes.

I wanted my mother to taste the healing, the peace of mind and forgiveness that I had witnessed in hundreds of other people. In retrospect, this was my need, not hers. Perhaps it was really a need of forgiveness before her death. But our track record for intimate conversation was poor, and discussion of our mutual feelings about life and death were no exception. We had no shared vocabulary for feelings. So for the most part, our conversations centered on politics, family, and sports.

Sitting in my mother's bedroom, watching television and making small talk, I continued to search for some way to make a deeper spiritual connection. One evening my former husband crawled into bed next to her, held her in his arms, and lovingly recounted inspiring near-death experiences we had heard. She pushed these away with good humor, commenting that we could believe in such things if it made us feel better, but they didn't speak to her in the least.

A few weeks before she died, Spirit provided an experience that spoke to her. Mom, an avid baseball fan, was a Bostonian, and the Red Sox were naturally her team. Like most of Boston, she had followed the saga of Wade Boggs, a third baseman, with great interest. Boggs's mistress had spilled to the newspaper some nasty gossip he had told her about his teammates, and he was publicly humiliated.

The media had a field day with his indiscretions. Even though I'm not a baseball fan, my attention was caught one day by a newspaper article that queried why Boggs was doing so well in the stressful situation. The answer was nothing short of astonishing. Boggs's mother had recently died, and he reported that she had come back to him as a full three-dimensional apparition! She assured him that we learn from our mistakes and that he should take responsibility for what he'd done and go on. At the same time, she had appeared to Boggs's sister, who was confined to a wheelchair with multiple sclerosis so advanced that even her vocal cords were paralyzed. She asked her daughter to give the eulogy at her funeral, and her daughter recovered sufficiently to do so!

Filled with the most delicious excitement, I phoned my mother and read her the article. For once she was speechless. Just a few weeks later, I was with her when she went into respiratory distress. I called an ambulance, and we rode through the snow to the hospital for the last time.

In the ER, a very kind nurse, whom she knew well from previous stays, told Mom that she was close to death and asked if she was at peace with that. Barely conscious up to this point, Mother was fairly resurrected with her own version of the good news. "Am I at peace with death?" she crowed. "Have you heard about Wade Boggs's mother?"

As she lay dying, Mom pondered the perennial questions in a new way. Never once did she question that her soul would live on—apparently the apparition of Mrs. Boggs convinced her of that. Instead, she pondered about whether my father, her brother, and her parents would be there on the other side to greet her. The hope of reunion gave her tremendous peace.

The morning of her death, she was taken down to the hospital basement, where the radiology department was located. She was bleeding internally, and they wanted to diagnose the source of the bleeding. When she had not reappeared after several hours, the family dispatched me to look for her. I found her alone, on a stretcher, in the hospital corridor. She was waiting her turn for X ray.

Although I'm not usually an assertive person, I lambasted the young doctor in charge and demanded that they let my mother go back to her room, where the family was waiting to say goodbye. He commented dryly that first they needed a diagnosis for her bleeding. Mom retorted, "You mean I've been waiting here all day for a diagnosis? Why didn't you just ask me. I'm dying—that's your diagnosis." He couldn't argue with her logic, and surprisingly he let her go.

I rode up in the elevator next to her stretcher. Holding hands on that brief ascent, we accomplished the work of a lifetime—the exchange of forgiveness and the realization of a deep mutual love.

JOAN BORYSENKO

Guts and Glory

To CELEBRATE MY FIFTIETH BIRTHDAY, I DECIDED TO buy a Harley-Davidson motorcycle, pack my sleeping bag and tent, and ride through all fifty states—one for each year of my life.

The blue-eyed, red-haired image in the mirror looked remarkably calm for a woman who had just made this life-changing decision. I knew I wanted to do something outrageous to celebrate my milestone, but there were still obstacles, fears, and doubts.

Preparing for a three-month adventure was no small undertaking. I had never been alone. After a marriage that lasted seventeen years, my two sons lived with me for the next ten. My oldest son was in college, and my nineteen-year-old would need to find a place to stay. I worried about his lack of experience and if he would be OK.

What about my law practice? After my divorce, at age forty, I earned a law degree and developed a successful practice. To walk away from this seemed almost irresponsible.

And then there was this important relationship. I loved the guy, but it was hard. I was tense much of the time. Our talks of commitment were always accompanied with that uncomfortable gut feeling. I began wondering if I was with him to compensate for my loneliness. That relentless inner voice knew our relationship would not survive the three-month separation.

Finally, I knew the woman who returned would not be the same woman who left. That bothered me. I rather liked the woman I was. A 14,200-mile journey alone through all fifty states would clearly be a life-changing event. In what ways would the trip change me? Would I even return?

Yet I had a lot going for me. Physically, I was in good shape. Mechanically, my bike was sound. I had confidence in the goodwill of the people I was sure to meet along the way. I also had an underlying confidence in myself.

To push through my veil of fear, I had to risk everything that was known and secure to me. I kept hearing in my mind the phrase: "Do the thing you fear, and death of fear is certain." So I took off on my long journey, including special side trips to Alaska and Hawaii.

My trip was magical! I felt as if I were living out a fantasy. I swam with the manatees in Florida, encountered a tarantula on my bathroom floor in Oklahoma, saw the high plains of Kansas, rode through howling winds in Montana, felt the magnificence of Bryce Canyon, and touched the glaciers of Alaska.

But the most important part was what happened within me. This trip put my life in perspective. My soul and spirit was fed. Inner peace and contentment replaced my fear of loneliness. I learned to treasure my time alone. My pace is slower now. No longer practicing law, I'm writing instead. My sons are beginning the adventure of their own lives.

I decided to move back to my rural home in Oregon to spend time with my parents. Before my trip, I would never have considered moving home. I now know that where we live is not as important as spending time with those we love.

While on the trip, I ended the relationship I'd been in, and we went our separate ways.

No longer driven by fear of loneliness, I met "Mr. Wonderful" in, of all places, that small hometown I once resisted. When I first saw him, he was leaning against his Harley-Davidson, surveying the crowd at a local bike rally. As I pulled off my helmet, our eyes met. I could tell what he was thinking: Is it really possible to meet a great woman who loves to ride Harleys?

We married months later, for all the right reasons. He calls me his "red-haired fox." As for the fifty-year-old woman who came back from her life-changing journey, she did change—and I like her even better!

CAROLYN FOX

✒

My Love Affair with Vladimir

MY SEARCH WAS ON FOR A CAR. I WALKED UP AND down the aisle, scrutinizing each one, waiting for a sign of recognition, a kindred spirit. Some were too old, too worn, and not well cared for. Some were too young, making me wonder, was there a problem? Then I spied my perfect match. We made contact, his grille forming a rakish grin. I grabbed my husband's arm. "Oh, Don, look!" I had to touch it. The salesman saw that look in my eyes. "I'll get the keys," he said, and went running back to his office. He unlocked the car, and I got in. My excitement grew as I stroked the steering wheel. Only 53,000 miles. Not bad. Burgundy with tan interior. I felt right at home—like it was meant to be. It was a done deal. I was now the proud owner of a three-year-old Volvo.

I've always been of the philosophy that one should name the car one drives. Makes the car feel important and establishes a bond between car and driver. I've come to believe that everything has a consciousness. Why treat your car any differently than you would treat your mother? I wanted my car to know the permanence of our union. I knew immediately that this car was male. Instinctively, I began to call him Vladimir.

One December I noticed other people putting wreaths on the front of their cars. (I think it's a Saint Louis thing, because I haven't seen this anywhere else.) I bought Vladimir a wreath as well. He wears it proudly every December and looks quite handsome. I felt he deserved even more, so for Halloween I bought him a companion—an inflatable skeleton, which I strap into the front passenger seat each October. Vladimir gets lots of other attention as well. He knows I love him—I praise him regularly and pat his dashboard each time we're together. I indulge him with other treats, like better gasoline, deluxe car washes, extra-rich leather cleaner—little things to make him feel special. My last purchase for Vladimir was a mini wind chime, designed to resonate peace and harmony, which I hung from the rearview mirror. The sound is divine.

My husband has made fun of me for years about my devotion to my car. He has a Volvo too—the same model as Vlad, but three years newer. To Don, his Volvo is "just a car," and he pays no attention to his car's physical or spiritual well-being. Don thinks the attention and gifts I lavish on Vladimir are nonsense. He jokingly calls Vladimir's half of the garage the "sacred half." But actions speak louder than words, and the results speak for themselves. Vladimir has needed only routine maintenance, while Don's car has had repeated mechanical problems—he even had to have the transmission rebuilt. Once, I drove his car home alone from a vacation, and it stopped running outside Joliet, Illinois. The car had to be towed to the local dealer and needed *both* fuel pumps replaced. I know in my heart that Vladimir would never do that to me.

Vladimir will be fourteen years old this year and has mileage well into the six digits. We've been together for eleven of those years, and he's never failed to take good care of me. His sense of purpose for service has been impeccable. Don and I looked at new Volvos recently. "He isn't going to last forever," Don snorted gruffly, but I just couldn't part with Vladimir.

Is it true what they say that love makes all things new again? I don't know. Vladimir doesn't look quite as bright and shiny as he once did, but his spirit is as vibrant as the day I drove him home. Looks like we'll be together until death do us part.

SHARON HYLL

❧

Sometimes You Can Go Back

GEORGE IS A BIG GUY. THE KIND OF FELLOW WHO might've been somebody's bodyguard, except that he has the personality of a big teddy bear. Recently retired and divorced, George came into my office to share a story with me about something that had happened to him.

"Reverend Mary," he said, "last Easter you told us that if we would let go of one habit that was limiting us, however small, in one year our life would be transformed. I want to tell you what happened to me.

"For most of my life, I've had a habit of biting the second knuckle on my index finger, like this." He bent the finger and put the knuckle between his teeth. "I even developed quite a callous on both sides of the finger. Well, I decided it was time to give that habit up. I've done pretty well at it all year—but let me give you a little background on this thing.

"When I was six years old, I saw my baby brother hit by a car and killed. He was two years younger than me. I had just run across that street, and he was following me. Just the day before, I was told to watch for cars and to look out for my little brother. We had been very close, and I was heartbroken.

"Sometime after that, I began to bite the back of my right hand between the knuckles of my first two fingers. I constantly had a callous there, about the size of a half-dollar. Whenever I felt angry or frustrated, I'd bite the top of that hand, right there on that spot.

"By the time I was a teenager, I guess I thought that was too childlike to do, and I switched to biting the one knuckle on my hand. I kept right on doing that until Easter of last year. After hearing your talk, I decided it was time to give up that habit.

"This year in March—almost one year after your Easter talk—I was spending the day with my grandson at the park. I noticed that I bit my knuckle that day. *How come?* I was also feeling a lot of love for my grandson as I watched him swing under his own locomotion.

"After I took him home, I went to visit some friends. I was feeling anxious that the laundry I'd meant to do was still in the trunk of my car. As I drove home that evening, my anxiety was rising. I was so rattled that I knew it had to be more than just the unfinished laundry. I had this huge knot in my stomach.

"I thought about my little grandson, who was just about the age my brother had been when he died. And I realized it was coming up on the anniversary of my brother's death, fifty-five years ago! I love that little guy so much, I thought to myself, and I'm afraid he'll be taken away. I knew right then that was just the way I'd felt when I lost my brother. I somehow had it wired up that loving my brother so much had caused me to lose him!

"But this last year, I was changing and not really seeing it. During that day in the park, I was expressing true love for my little grandson —more love than I'd given to my five kids and both my former wives.

"Since that day, I've shared this story with all of them. I've tried to make amends for all the love that I withheld from my family all these years—for fear I'd lose them.

"Reverend Mary, I know if I was still biting this knuckle every time I felt mad, or sad, or frustrated, I wouldn't have uncovered any of this. It was giving up that one habit that taught me so much and let all this love come to the surface. So you see, when you told us our lives would be transformed in one year by taking one little action, you were so right!

"I've been officially retired since the first of May, but now I'm really ready to be retired. This summer I'm just going to play with my grandson. I feel like I've finally got my little brother back!"

REV. MARY MURRAY SHELTON

𝒥𝒫

No Mistakes Here

❦

I'S NOT EASY BEING MARRIED TO SOMEONE WHO HAS never made a mistake. My husband, Bud, is constitutionally incapable of admitting that he has ever been wrong. I don't think his mouth can form the words "I'm sorry. I made a mistake."

This aspect of his personality is best illustrated by an incident that happened recently.

I was on the phone one evening, talking with my brother, when he asked, "Did Bud tell you I called last night?"

I turned to Bud and said, "Honey, you didn't tell me my brother called last night."

Without interrupting his concentration or even shifting his eyes from the TV set, my husband answered, "Not yet."

ANITA CHEEK MILNER

❦

"When work, commitment, and pleasure all become one and you reach that deep well where passion lives, nothing is impossible."

—Nancy Coey

You'll Be an Artist When You Grow Up

I'VE ALWAYS BEEN FASCINATED WITH COLOR. AS A child, I loved to paint and draw with crayons. To my preschool mind, every picture I created was a masterpiece! Then I went to the first grade.

We were asked one day to color pictures, which would be given to the residents of a nursing home to brighten their day. Every child was given one sheet to color. We were also told that a few extra were needed, and anyone who finished early and had done a good job could color more than one. I *wanted* to color more than one. I quickly colored the design with lots of bright colors and raised my hand, sure that my paper would be good enough for me to color another one.

When my teacher came over to look at my work, she scolded me in a loud voice. "Kathleen, that paper is awful. You used too many colors and couldn't even stay in the lines!" I was crushed. I didn't get to color another paper and was forced to sit quietly, holding in my embarrassment, as the rest of the class completed the project.

After that day, I stopped drawing pictures. I dreaded the art class that had been my favorite part of school. Each time I was forced to do anything artistic, I cringed and retreated inside myself. To this day, I do not remember any art project completed after the day my teacher made me feel incompetent and unartistic, although I can tell you all about the many projects I'd completed before that day.

About four years later, our family had a visit from an elderly friend of my mother's. She was a delightful woman, and I spent hours talking to her. Art or creativity was never mentioned. A short while later, my mother received a letter from her friend, thanking her for our hospitality.

The letter contained a paragraph about all of the children in my family. She told my mother how wonderful she thought each of us was, and she proceeded to list what careers she thought we would have when we grew up. I don't remember what was predicted for any of my brothers or sisters, but I'll never forget the feeling of warmth that passed over me as my mother read the letter aloud. It said that I would be an artist when I grew up. An artist!

That afternoon I dug out my old box of crayons and drawing paper. I drew everything I could, nonstop, in every spare minute for the next month. I stopped drawing one day and looked back over all I had created. It looked pretty good, I thought. Good enough that I wished I could show it to my first-grade teacher.

My rekindled artistic spirit eventually took on many new forms and expressions. Today, I travel the world and teach thousands of people a year how to be more creative, how to design beautiful projects, and how to use color in their businesses and their lives. I've written thirty books on the subject and have had hundreds of articles printed. I've even been featured on fifteen videos, have my own television show, and have appeared on numerous other programs.

How different my life, and the lives of those I touch creatively each year, would be if an elderly woman I met only once in my life hadn't told me I'd be an artist when I grew up! She taught me an important life lesson: to honor each person's unique artistic talents. I now encourage others and teach them to color outside the lines.

KATHY LAMANCUSA

✍

VIII

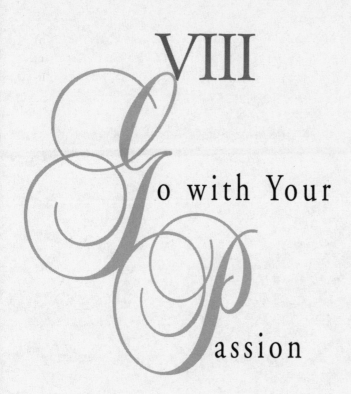

Go with Your Passion

*"You are your own promised land,
your own new frontier."*

—Julia Cameron

The Dreamer

W HEN I WAS NINE YEARS OLD, LIVING IN A SMALL town in North Carolina, I found an ad for selling greeting cards in the back of a children's magazine. I thought to myself: I can do this. I begged my mother to let me send for the kit.

Two weeks later, when the kit arrived, I ripped off the brown paper wrapper, grabbed the cards, and dashed from the house. Three hours later, I returned home with no cards and a pocket full of money, proclaiming, "Mama, all the people couldn't wait to buy my cards!"

A salesperson was born.

When I was twelve years old, my father took me to see Zig Ziglar. I remember sitting in that dark auditorium, listening to Mr. Ziglar raise everyone's spirits to the ceiling. I left there feeling I could do anything. When we got to the car, I turned to my father and said, "Dad, I want to make people feel like that." My father asked me what I meant. "I want to be a motivational speaker, just like Mr. Ziglar," I replied.

A dream was born.

Recently, I began pursuing my dream of motivating others. After a four-year relationship with a major Fortune 100 company, beginning as a sales trainer and ending as a regional sales manager, I left the company at the height of my career. Many people were astounded that I would leave after earning a six-figure income, and they asked why I would risk everything for a dream.

I made my decision to start my own company and leave my secure position after attending a regional sales meeting. There, the vice president of our company delivered a speech that changed my life. He asked us, "If a genie would grant you three wishes, what would they be?" After giving us a moment to write down the three wishes, he then asked, "Why do you need a genie?" I will never forget the empowerment I felt at that moment!

I realized that everything I had accomplished: the graduate degree, the successful sales career, speaking engagements, training and managing for a Fortune 100 company—had prepared me for this moment. I was ready and did not need a genie's help to become a motivational speaker. When I tearfully told my boss my plans, this incredible leader whom I respect so much replied, "Proceed with reckless abandon and you will be successful."

Having made that decision, I was immediately tested. One week after I gave notice, my husband was laid off from his job. We had recently bought a new home and needed both incomes to make the monthly mortgage payment, and now we were down to no income. It was tempting to turn back to my former company, knowing they wanted me to stay. But I was certain that if I went back, I'd never leave. I decided I still wanted to move forward rather than end up with a mouthful of "if onlys" later on.

A motivational speaker was born.

When I held fast to my dream, even during the tough times, the miracles really began to happen. In a short time period, my husband found a better job, we didn't miss a mortgage payment, and I was able to book several speaking engagements with new clients. I discovered the incredible power of dreams.

I loved my old job, my peers, and the company I left, but it was time to get on with my dream. To celebrate my success, I had a local artist paint my new office to resemble a garden. At the top of one wall she stenciled, "The World Always Makes Way for the Dreamer."

APRIL KEMP

✒

"Only those who see the invisible
can do the impossible."

—Author unknown

Paddling Upstream

CHILDREN HAVE ALWAYS BEEN AN IMPORTANT PART
of my life. As a kindergarten teacher for twenty-eight years, I was
surrounded by children—other people's children, for I'd had none of
my own.

In my married life, twenty-five years ago, we tried to have children.
After my divorce, I tried artificial insemination. Still no baby. To someone who had always been drawn to motherhood, it was all the more
heartbreaking when it never happened.

Feeling as though I was desperately running out of time, I decided it
was time to really get serious! This was going to happen. Period. I was
going to take *every* step necessary to have a baby. Every time I came to an
obstacle, I would get past it. Deep inside, I knew I would be a mom.

I retired from teaching and devoted myself to preparing for motherhood. Although the physicians in the fertility clinic said my chances
were growing slimmer, I surrounded myself with people who supported
my dream. I didn't give up even when I felt I was paddling upstream
against a strong current.

Using money from my early retirement, I funded an embryo transfer. While a donor egg was readily available, the sperm proved trickier. I fearfully approached a man I'd been dating a short time. I remember how awkward and emotional I felt telling him about my dream. I asked him to donate his sperm. Tears welled in his eyes. Rather than run, he was honored to be a part of my passionate quest.

I continued dreaming of having a child. I meditated about having a child. I created affirmations like "I am healthy, happy, and pregnant!" I made a huge poster covered with photographs of babies and pregnant women. It was in a prominent place in my home, so everyone who came in could see and believe with me.

The embryo implantation was successful—I did not expect anything other than that! My pregnancy was problem free. The C-section went smoothly, and on March 29, 1995, Zachary Lee Roth entered my life.

There's an analogy I strongly relate to. I'm like a salmon. The salmon has one goal: to get back to that spawning ground and lay her eggs. It will thrash through the rapids and over the rocks. It gets battered, but not beaten. No matter what, that determined salmon will get there or die. I'm definitely that salmon—and I made it!

I'm hard to reach these days. I'm busy playing with my young son. It's a miracle to watch him grow and change each day. It's a miracle I'm on my own, yet able to create this beautiful young child.

When I got to that place where I could see what I had to have, nothing could stop me. Having a baby was miracle enough. What made it a major miracle was having my baby at age fifty.

HARRIET ROTH

164

The Magic of Anger

SUDDENLY THE CLASSROOM DOOR FLEW OPEN. IN MARCHED the vice principal, better known as "The Tyrant." You could hear an undercurrent of groans as The Tyrant folded her arms in front of her buxom bosom and lifted one eyebrow so high it looked as if it could emerge from the crown of her cranium. The Tyrant was no ordinary lady. In fact, she was no lady at all, but rather the epitome of "I'm Not OK; and Neither Are You."

I pondered what game she was about to play, as I attempted to carry on with my lesson. My students were enthusiastically involved in a discussion of a popular psychology of the day, based on Thomas Harris's *I'm O.K., You're O.K.* and Eric Berne's *Games People Play.* I really loved interacting with my students and had become their "noon-hour counselor."

Instead of watching the dynamics of the class, The Tyrant fixed her icy stare at me. After a grueling thirty minutes of intense scrutiny, she got up and started to walk out. We were all primed for a huge sigh of relief, when she suddenly did an about-face and lurched at me. Her jaw was clenched, and she wildly jabbed her finger in fury, preparing to dissect her victim of the day. She snarled with such vengeance that I could taste her bitter breath. "Who do you think you are, Mrs. Field? Watch what you say to these students. Remember, you are not a psychologist."

As the anger welled up inside me, it felt as though my blood pressure soared beyond the measure of any instrument. My adrenaline surged and my pulse skyrocketed. My eyes filled with tears, and my heart beat to the frenzy of a primitive war dance. It was all I could do to keep a lid on my boiling insides.

165

After The Tyrant had completed her abusive mission and finally stalked out, the students rallied to my defense. One cried, "She shouldn't be let out without a keeper!" Another added, "She needs to be tamed. She took apart my purse today in the lavatory, even though I asked her to stop because I don't do cigs or drugs." It was the quavering voice of a usually shy boy that really got to me. "She's just jealous because we come to you with our problems instead of her."

As I drove home that evening, still feeling like Mount Vesuvius ready for the grand eruption, the stored-up tears flowed like hot lava that burned without comfort. When I finally crawled into bed, I could not sleep. Over and over again, the taunting words of The Tyrant resounded: *Remember, you are not a psychologist. Who do you think you are? You are not a psychologist. You are not . . ."*

The endless night finally gave way to a brilliant dawn. As the morning star illuminated my face, a light went on in my brain, and I heard myself shout, "Why *not* a psychologist?" Passion replaced my anger, and I found myself in the car, driving to the university. Before the sun gave way to the full moon, I had registered for my first course in clinical psychology.

Our teachers come in many forms. Sometimes we are jolted toward change by those least likely to have a positive impact. The Tyrant, in her quest to quench my spirit and put me in my place, failed at the first task while succeeding brilliantly at the second. My spirit soared as the fire of my anger became the fuel for my newly chosen path.

Many years have passed since that transition in my life. Yesterday, the door of my office opened. In walked a new patient, looking like a teakettle ready to steam. "Dr. Field," she said, her eyes filled with tears, "I'm a schoolteacher. I've had such a terrible day. I have this tyrannical principal. She bawled me out in front of the whole class. I'm so humiliated. I can't take it anymore!"

Compassion welled up within me as I said, "I believe I can help you."

ELEANOR S. FIELD

❧

An Influential Lunch Date

JP

I WORE A RED PLAID PLEATED SKIRT, A WHITE BLOUSE with a Peter Pan collar, white bobby socks, and penny loafers at the Cathedral of Saint Raymond's school. In the sixth grade, I was convinced I knew exactly how our school should run. I was frustrated by the lack of school spirit. I decided it was my mission to save the school.

At the end of a crisp autumn day, I marched down to the principal's office and asked the ancient secretary to see Sister Muriel. Looking very stern in her drab gray suit, Sister Muriel asked what I needed. Words spilled out of me about how we needed more school spirit. She cut me off and asked if I would join her for lunch the next day. Obviously she recognized my keen intellect! There was a bounce in my step the whole way home.

"I'm having lunch with the principal!" I declared to my friends. "Are you in trouble?" "How boring!" exclaimed my pals. As usual, my friends thought I was insane. They thought only teachers could change things like school spirit.

Sister Muriel had pulled a huge red leather chair next to the desk for me. Once I climbed up, my toes barely touched the floor. Carefully, I spread my napkin over the desk and arranged my baloney sandwich, Cheetos, and a carton of chocolate milk. Sister Muriel had done the same with her tuna fish sandwich, pretzels, and Oreos. I couldn't believe a nun ate Oreos!

While munching on pretzels, Sister Muriel asked me to explain, in detail, my concerns. I rambled passionately on about school spirit. After several minutes, she leaned forward and asked, "What do you

167

want to do about it?" Uh-oh. I didn't know. Slowly, I began to give her ideas—ending each one with a question mark in my voice. After each proposal, she would ask me, "What resources can we use? How would we carry it out? Would the other students support it?" Together we weeded out the silly ideas and elaborated on the good ones. Once we identified three strong prospects, she asked me to pick my favorite one. Sister Muriel leaned back in her chair and asked me if I was really committed to this project. With the enthusiasm of an innocent child, I exclaimed, "Yes, Sister!" She looked me straight in the eye and said, "OK, you can do this." I believe I flew home that day.

Over the next three years, I ate many lunches while sitting in that huge red chair. Sister Muriel made me feel important. With each lunch, I expressed myself better. I learned to predict what she might ask. It became a game to see how prepared I could be. Eventually I was able to come to lunch with a few solid ideas and an action plan. Sister Muriel listened to me, let me try things, let me fail, and let me try again. I thought I knew everything going into those lunches. But it was during those lunches that I learned everything.

Much later, as a first-year teacher, I was convinced that I knew exactly how the school should be run. Deeply concerned about the lack of school spirit, I decided it was my mission to save our school. Armed with ideas, I flew into my principal's office. "Tom, we must have lunch!" I exclaimed. The next day, we sat together over lunch and discussed my ideas. We agreed on a plan, and Tom gave me a green light. I believe I flew back to my classroom.

When I casually mentioned to a tenured teacher that I was going to see Tom, she explained to me that principals are very busy people, that teachers can't really change anything, only administrators can cause change. I thanked her for her insight and went to see Tom anyway. Over the years, Tom and I have become good friends. He's encouraged my confidence to share ideas with him.

Looking back now, I'm grateful that Sister Muriel and Tom took the time to listen to an enthusiastic young person. I know they were very busy, yet they still found time for me. There are moments in time that create who we are. It is from these moments that confidence is created or destroyed.

I have come to believe that anyone, regardless of age or position, can offer ideas and cause change. I hope that someday someone comes to me with an idea, and I am able to invite that individual to lunch.

MARGUERITE MURER

৶৶

Shut Up and Dance

ॐ

ARTHA GRAHAM, THE HIGH PRIESTESS OF MODERN dance in America, once said, "I am a dancer, and I believe that we learn by practice—whether that means we learn to dance by practicing dance or learn to live by practicing living. Life does not have to be interpreted—it has to be experienced."

I studied dance for years. I would come to class early and spend an hour or more warming up and striking regal poses for the admiring mirrors on the studio walls. I marveled at my perfect alignment and fabulous extensions. The analytical interpretation and technical perfection held me spellbound. Alone in that studio, I was Margot Fonteyn dancing a pas de deux with Rudolf Nureyev. . . . I was Isadora Duncan, scarves flying, scandalizing all of Europe with her sensual interpretations.

Yes. In my imagination, I was awesome!

Until class began.

Then the admiring mirrors turned into leering spectators. I'd catch a glimpse of my less-than-perfect image, and cringe and gasp at what I saw. With all the students' eyes upon me, I changed from a prima ballerina to an awkward student.

Can you relate? Have you ever fancied yourself Pavarotti or Maria Callas in the shower, but outside of that steamy chamber you'd be mortified to even chime in on a chorus of "Happy Birthday"?

Frustrated, my dance teacher would turn to me and say, "Mari Pat, you must give yourself up to the movement—dance full out—unafraid of the consequences!"

170

I would nod, pretend I understood, and once again timidly take my place on the dance floor. This went on for months.

Because cold muscles are dangerous for a dancer, we arrived at the studio during winter bundled from head to toe. As we worked and warmed up, our clothes came off in layers. One day we'd been working at the barre for about an hour when a fellow dance student stripped off his sweatshirt, to reveal a T-shirt emblazoned with his life philosophy. The words across his chest shouted: SHUT UP AND DANCE.

I was so stunned that I nearly collided with him. The words pierced me like a thunderbolt. So simple! So true!

At that moment, I learned that life is happening right now. This is the real thing! It's time to stop planning, posturing, and postponing. It's time to stop *talking* about a dream—and start *doing* my dream. I finally let go of my negative self talk and striving for perfection. I released my inner music. On that day, I became a dancer.

MARI PAT VARGA

"When you hold back on life,
life holds back on you."

—Mary Manin Morrissey

Someday

ঔ৶৹

ID YOU EVER KNOW ANYONE WHO HAD A DREAM SO infectious that everyone believed in it? I had a friend like that in college.

Suzy Brown was a beautiful, bouncy blonde with huge flashing green eyes and a laugh that could stop a rainstorm. She wanted to be a clown —a real live Barnum & Bailey clown—and she practiced every day. Suzy would dress up in funny old clothes, turn somersaults, lean backward until I thought she would break, and strut around the room, singing, "I've a bright-red nose, big shoes of brown, and I will be the world's best clown!"

And she might have been . . . if she had tried.

When I saw Suzy a few years later, she was not in the center ring, not wearing a polka-dot suit, not making people laugh. She was living alone in a tiny apartment, tied to a low-paying job that she hated and too busy to see the circus when it came to town. She was twenty-five years old, but she seemed sixty-five. You know what she said? She said, "It's not over, Kay. Someday I'll have another chance. Someday I'll go to the circus. Someday when . . ."

Like Suzy, I had a dream. My dream was to be a speaker who could inspire people to do and be whatever they wanted. But first I needed

172

the confidence to stand in a room filled with people, open my mouth, and have something . . . anything . . . come out. But I was so scared, I couldn't lead a silent prayer! My brain may have started working the day I was born, but it sure stopped when I tried to speak in public!

For years, I said I wanted to develop my speaking skills. But I was busy, I was broke, I was sick, I didn't know how. When you're afraid to do something, one excuse is just as good as another.

One day, after telling so many others about my dream and preparing for it for so long in little ways I didn't even recognize, I ran out of excuses. I knew I *had* to walk through my fear of speaking.

The first time I tried to make a speech, there were only ten people in the room, and I knew every one of them well. I also knew my speech well, but when I stood up to speak, every function in my body failed. My memory stopped. My eyes glazed over, and I couldn't see my audience anymore. My heart tried to pound its way out of my chest. My body went into rigor mortis. My deodorant stopped working! I took a deep breath, became light-headed, faced my friends—and very calmly fainted!

Ever so slowly, I *did* learn to speak. I even won a few speech contests. With every success, I became braver. And with every loss, I became stronger. I eventually became a finalist in the International Championship of Public Speaking!

Remember my friend Suzy Brown? My beautiful and talented friend died of cancer at the age of thirty, without ever being part of the circus. Her "someday" never came. The last time I saw her, she said, "Kay, I only wish I had another chance to try." Putting your dreams on hold is like putting your life on hold.

Two dreams . . . two endings . . . I took the first step, Suzy put her dream on hold. If Suzy could talk to us right now, I'll bet she'd say, "Don't be afraid to reach for the stars; that's why God put them out so far."

KAY duPONT

173

IX

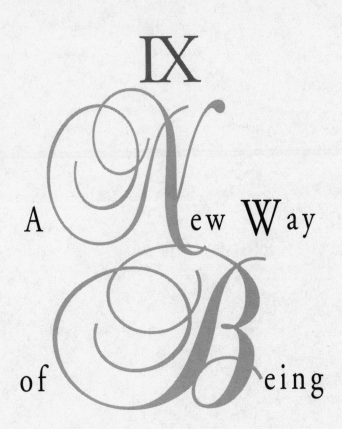

A New Way of Being

𝔍𝔍

*"You cannot discover new oceans, unless you
have the courage to lose sight of the shore."*

—Author unknown

You Don't Have to Come Home from Work Exhausted!

ᏍᎵᏋ

STUDYING WITH DR. MARGARET MEAD, I NOTICED THAT she enjoyed a different quality of energy. She worked circles around the rest of us, even though she was thirty-five to forty years our senior! One day I asked, "Margaret, how can you enjoy such abundant energy, when the rest of us are dragging?"

She stopped and thought for a moment, scratching her head as she did so, then replied with a grin, "I suppose it's because I never grew up . . . while fooling most people into believing that I have!"

Taking what she said to heart, I began to sift through the joy of my childhood. Just remembering playing kick the can on a summer's night would revive me with that special energy we all experienced as kids.

So what might happen if I got even bolder and claimed some precious dreams that never happened? I never told anyone I wanted tap-dance lessons as a child, wanted to dance in a recital wearing a beautiful costume and shiny black tap shoes.

I grew up in Houston, next door to an adorable little girl named Linda Hovey. She was petite and looked a lot like Shirley Temple. I was big, gawky, and teased with the nickname "Miss Moose" by my older brother and his friends.

So, years later, it took all the courage I could muster to go into a neighborhood shoe store and order size 9B tap shoes.

"How old is the kid with 9B feet?" the clerk asked with amazement.

"Soon she will be fifty," I answered in a quiet, embarrassed voice.

Late at night, after my family went to bed, I would put on a videotape by Bonnie Franklin called *Let's Tap* and claim my fantasy of becoming Shirley Temple onstage.

One night my husband, Larry, woke up and came through the den on his way to the kitchen for a bowl of Grape-Nuts. Catching me in the act, he said, "Hey, you're almost good at it!" We both laughed, and I shared my ideas about living our dreams. He had enjoyed playing the saxophone and clarinet as a boy, so we searched through the want ads and found a wonderful old clarinet.

We were absolutely amazed that we could come home from our workday totally drained and exhausted, yet after twenty minutes of music for Larry and a few shuffle-ball changes for me, we both would experience a miraculous rejuvenation. Inspired by our discovery, we decided to give ourselves a surprise 104th birthday party (his fifty-fourth and my fiftieth). The surprise would be a joint recital, and all our friends would be invited to perform something they enjoyed as a kid or dreamed of doing.

We couldn't believe the energy that led up to that magical night. Friends arrived with costumes, props, and scripts, surrounded by mystery. Like young children, we each fought the delicate balance of fear tinged with excitement as we waited our turn to perform. Ordinarily, when adults perform, we expect to have rehearsed until we are perfect. But kids rehearse until they are bored or tired and then say, "Pretend I'm really good!" That night we pretended, and we clapped wildly for each other.

In the ten years since that life-changing night, I have risked sharing my childhood dream and dared to tap-dance badly for many audiences. They delight in my childlike courage as I ask for a standing ovation at the end, "like you might give Barbra Streisand when she was the best she has ever been." There are always tears in the crowd, our kid selves begging us to make room for them in our busy lives.

When I do these outrageous performances, I end with a childhood game, I Dare You! I say, "I dare you to spend some time with childhood dreams and fantasies. Then find your own creative way to claim them."

One very dignified, six-foot-six CEO thanked me after I received a standing ovation at his company's annual meeting. "All my life I have secretly wished I could tap-dance," he said. "I'll soon be sixty-eight, and today you've given me the courage to claim that lifelong dream!"

ANN McGEE-COOPER

❧

From Under the Boot Heel

JP

IN MY TWENTY YEARS AS A PARAMEDIC, I HAVE BEEN charged with performing duties that require enormous amounts of bravery. I was about to learn a new kind.

Several years ago, I sat in a dilapidated office housed in a condemned hospital building in the center of a nondescript town in south Texas. I lit a cigarette (this was back in the days when one could smoke in a building) and watched a large cockroach climb up the wall in front of my desk. I began my 457th day of acute self-pity.

Tim, an EMT coworker, strolled in and flicked the ugly bug onto the floor, slamming down on it with the heavy heel of a patrol boot. Even with that pounding, the bug wouldn't die. Sort of like me, I thought. Stomped on unmercifully, and I keep coming back for more.

In the year since my divorce, there had been few happy days. My entire existence seemed to depend solely on my life-saving duties. Responding to an emergency was the only time I knew my heart was beating. My thoughts turned once more to the core of my problem. *If only I could find a nice man . . .*

I suddenly felt ill. What was I thinking? Am I to waste my entire life waiting for Prince Charming? He certainly had not been around during the first thirty-seven years.

I stood up and walked past Tim and out to the street. Standing on the curb, I surveyed my surroundings. "Oh my God!" I said to myself while continuing my slow turn. "There is nothing to see here, no view, no green trees or water, no spiky mountains. Not even a hill. Why am

I here?" The question was the internal combustion I needed. I smiled and felt hope welling up within me. Standing there on the curb of Center Street, dressed in my uniform, I laughed until tears streaked my face.

That night I pulled out a yellow legal pad. On it I wrote: "WHAT I WANT." Under the heading, I listed eight items: 1. to live in a beautiful place with a 360-degree view; 2. to make a good salary; 3. to once again own a red sports car; 4. to never see a cockroach again; 5. to have a wonderful job teaching EMTs and paramedics; 6. to be proud of myself; 7. to never, *ever* need a man again, except for plumbing repairs; 8. to spend my next forty years in peace and happiness. I worked until the wee hours of the morning, polishing my résumé, and then I sent copies to Emergency Medical Services offices in four northwestern states.

Over fifty people attended my going-away party, and each of them asked the same question. "Wendy, how can you just pack up and go to Alaska without knowing anyone there?" Some of the women said, "I could never go off to the wilderness all alone." One man informed me that there were seven men to one woman in Alaska. "You're going to get a husband, right?"

"Yeah, right."

The truth is, I had chosen to enjoy my own company for a while. Something I had never really done.

In one week, I would become the Emergency Medical Services Coordinator for Southeast Alaska. The job required travel by boat and float plane to outlying areas—the bush. I was to spend time in these isolated communities teaching classes on emergency services. I never knew such a career existed, and it was as if I had designed the position myself.

As I looked around at all the doubting faces that day, I felt absolutely no fear. Just joy. Two suitcases and four boxes of training materials were all I had packed. I purged myself of all belongings.

As I said my goodbyes, I realized it took no bravery to pack up and move to Alaska. The bravery had occurred when I made my list and resolved to fulfill it. I recognized that I could control my own destiny. The weakness was in waiting for change instead of creating it.

Who do I need? Me. Who do I depend on? Me. Who do I love? Me. Who makes me happy? Me. Selfish, you say. Darned right. And there are no cockroaches in Alaska.

WENDY NATKONG

ℑ

Firewalk—Warming My "Soul"

§

MY FRIEND ROBERT PHONED TO SAY HE'D JUST EXPE-rienced a "firewalk." Excited, he encouraged me to do it too, saying, "It was amazingly easy—like walking through a doorway of fear." I was impressed with Robert's personal triumph of "mind over matter."

I had spent years believing I wouldn't achieve results unless I was willing to roll a large boulder uphill in the process. Maybe this walk was just the boost I needed.

The workshop began with the lighting of a huge pile of wood. The temperature of the wood would reach 1200–1300 degrees. That's hot enough to melt aluminum. Yet we were expected to walk on the glowing embers barefoot without burning our feet!

We were instructed to become aware of our body sensations and our thoughts, to *know* whether or not it was safe for us to walk across the embers. If we noticed our body was tense, or we thought: I'm afraid I will be burned, we shouldn't walk. If, however, our body and mind felt relaxed, and we thought: Yes, I trust I'll be safe, then we could go for it. We were being taught to trust our intuition.

A visualization process turned out to be the most revealing part of the evening. We were asked to think about any fears we might have about walking on fire and to visualize our *worst* fear realized. In my mind, I imagined my feet severely burned, but I was shocked to realize that wasn't my *worst* fear. My worst fear was of lying in a hospital bed, explaining to my sister how I had got burned. I was *really* afraid of what she would think of me. I could hear her exclaim, "Frances, why in the world did you pull this crazy, stupid stunt?" I had never known I cared so much about what other people thought of me.

We were then asked to visualize what would happen after we faced our worst fear. I experienced telling my sister what I had done and why. I saw her comforting me and expressing her love. Another revelation. Of course she would love me no matter what!

The firewalk instructor gave us four simple, yet very important, steps to follow for crossing the coals without getting burned (and for living our lives):

1. Know where you're starting from.

2. Know where you want to go.

3. Design a plan to get you there.

4. Follow the plan.

It was time to go outdoors and face the fire. "Am I going to trust my intuition, or am I going to hold back in fear?" I asked myself. I stood there feeling worn out, discouraged, and defeated from years of holding myself back. I was determined to break free! I made the commitment to trust myself and walk.

With that first step, I changed my life. I could feel a release as I stepped forward. I was doing what I wanted to do without the fear of what others would say. I proved to myself that fear doesn't have to stop me from being who I want to be. This was a breakthrough—I was actually walking barefoot on red-hot coals.

My feet began to feel very hot as I completed this powerful walk and stepped off onto the cool, wet grass. I used the garden hose to wash off the ash and cinders and went indoors, where I could examine my feet in the light. They were not burned or blistered at all. My intuition had served me well.

Since the firewalk, I have been more aware of the signals in my body and my mind whenever I need to make a decision or take a risk. My intuition has become a useful tool for making even the smallest choices in my life.

When my heart speaks now, I always listen. I check in with my intuition and design a plan I can follow. Each step of the way, I make sure I'm staying on track. I accomplish my innermost desires and experience much more ease and harmony in my life.

Yesterday I walked with fear. The firewalk warmed my soul and rekindled my spirit. Today I walk with confidence and joy, and amazing miracles have become a regular part of my life!

FRAN FISHER

∽

"Every time you heal a part of yourself,
you bring more light into the world."

—Author unknown

Doorway of Destiny

❧

IT WAS 10:30 A.M., AND I WAS ALREADY LATE FOR MY appointment. I had a busy day ahead of me; my mind was cluttered with the many tasks I wanted to accomplish. As I hurried down the crowded street in Seattle's Pioneer Square district, oblivious to my surroundings, I suddenly stopped, cemented in my tracks. Out of the corner of my eye, I noticed a flash of gold. Very slowly, life as I had known it began to change, and I was about to step from one field of reality to another.

I stood there with my heart pounding and my body sweating. I was unable to continue onward. Looking around, I saw nothing unusual—only a dirty brick building and a man curled up in the doorway. I didn't recognize him at first. In fact, it took me a few moments to figure out why I even stopped.

I never would have known him by the long, salt-and-pepper hair and scraggly beard. The torn gold polyester shirt and dirty brown pants were unfamiliar to me. I had never seen the ripped shoes and green military overcoat he had rolled himself in to keep warm.

186

The gold ring had caught my attention. His hand clung to the coat he was using as a blanket. The sunlight caused the ring to flash just as I walked by. How well I remembered that gold signet ring. I had seen it daily as a child.

Slowly, I realized the man sleeping in the doorway was my father. *My dad.* As I looked at this man whose ears and neck were covered with lice, memories of a handsome, charming man came flooding back. I remembered how much he was sought after as a dance partner at elite country club dances. I recalled how important it was for him to be immaculate, clean-shaven, and fashionably dressed.

It was as though a movie of my life passed in front of my eyes. I remembered the many parties; heard people laughing, drinking, and pretending. I also recalled the violent fights at the dinner table, night after night. The incest. The sarcasm. My parents' divorce. I remembered the good times. I saw Dad as we found the golden Easter egg at the club. The poem we wrote that won the honor of being published. Dad's remarriage. The private school. I saw the treatment center and felt the hope of recovery. It all flashed before me.

I stood there, grief-stricken and ashamed as the memories of yesterday came flooding back. I felt again the humiliation and embarrassment I had felt for so long. Angrily I asked, "Why, God, why my family? What's the purpose of all this? Why was my family hit so hard with alcoholism, drugs, and abuse? Why?"

I stood there, looking at my father, with tears running down my face. The depth of pain seemed unbearable, and yet it was in this moment that I surrendered. I began to experience the most freeing and healing moment of my life.

I began to understand. Before me was an eloquent expression of a life that had rediscovered its own soul. I believe we each choose our journey and discover what life is about in our own way. Others cannot do that for us.

I had spent years analyzing, criticizing, judging, and condemning my father. I had focused on trying to change him.

In that moment of truth, I began to understand that it was I who needed to change. I needed to move from holding on to letting go. I needed to move from judgment to compassion. I needed to honor his path of discovery. I needed to see both of us differently.

My father is one of the most talented and creative men I have ever known. His pathway of self-discovery was alcoholism, abuse, and, now, living on the street.

In that moment, I asked myself if I was willing to acknowledge my God-given creative talents and step boldly into my greatness. Or was I going to let bad habits, alcohol, and fear of others' opinions rob me of my dreams.

Although I was badly shaken, I continued to look at the gifted man curled up in the doorway. I realized it is not about right or wrong, should and should not. We each choose our response to life's challenges and learn what we learn.

I took one last look at my father lying in the doorway, wiped my tears, and whispered to myself, "Thanks, Dad, for teaching me about compassion."

JODY MILLER STEVENSON

He Loves Me, He Loves Me Not?

*"*D*AVE NEVER TELLS ME HE LOVES ME. SOMETIMES I don't think he even cares," my good friend Bonnie told me over lunch.

Knowing the couple well, I told her, "Bonnie, he really adores you. It's obvious."

"You really think so? After twenty-seven years of marriage, things aren't like they were the first year or two."

"I know how you feel, but why don't you try something?" I asked. "When you get home, start looking for evidence that he adores you instead of evidence to prove he doesn't. Just for twenty-four hours. OK?" Bonnie was quick to agree.

Bonnie phoned me the next day. "Your idea worked," she almost shouted. "When I got home, Dave asked, 'How was your lunch?' I thought to myself: He wants to know because he adores me. When he called me to come see the sunset, I thought: He's doing this because he adores me. In the middle of the night, I woke up and couldn't get back to sleep. Dave asked if anything was wrong and started rubbing my back.

"Some funny things started to happen. First, I noticed what a great guy he was. How else are you going to feel toward someone who adores you? And *then*, a little later, when he was grumpy, I thought: He's grumpy, but that's all right, because I know he adores me."

"Good for you," I said.

"Wait. There's more. I began to feel differently about myself too. I'm not such a bad person. In fact, I'm adorable." She giggled.

Bonnie learned she had the power to alter her perceptions. She could have gone home to the same old marriage, with her same old attitude, and things would have looked the same old way. Because she would have been looking to confirm he didn't love her, Bonnie would have missed all the love that was there.

Once, Bonnie used to ask, "Does he love me? Or does he love me not?" Now she is amazed to discover all the creative ways her husband finds to give her the answer that was there all along: "He loves me."

CHRISTINE B. EVANS

❧

"When we dim our light, we invite mediocrity."

—Kris King

What Do You Want to Do with the Rest of Your Life?

I'LL NEVER FORGET MY COLLEGE GUIDANCE COUN-selor, Cathy Martin. I met her when I transferred to Northwestern University as a sophomore.

Cathy invited me into her office and asked, "What do you want to do?"

I thought I was ready to respond boldly to the question. Proudly I announced, "I want to be in broadcasting."

Cathy seemed unimpressed by my declaration. She asked, "What, specifically, do you want to do in broadcasting?"

"I'll do anything."

"So will a lot of other people," she said sharply. "Broadcasting is a very competitive field. You need to know exactly what you want to do in order to succeed. You need to decide right here and now what it is you want to do."

I looked Cathy squarely in the eyes and stated with conviction, "I want to be a television news anchor and reporter."

She smiled. "Good," she said. "Now you know what you want to do. When you leave here, you tell everyone who you know what you want to do with your life—that you want to be a TV anchor and reporter. And on those days when you're feeling uncertain, you share that uncertainty with your family, with your friends, with me. But as to the rest of the world, you address them with certainty in all that you do."

I walked out of Cathy Martin's office. I had direction. I had a mission—to become a broadcast journalist *extraordinaire*. In December 1973, I graduated half a year early, to get a jump on the June graduates. Within several months, after countless rejections, I got that first job as a TV reporter. In fact, I was almost the first, as well as the youngest, female coanchor in the United States at the time. I went on to become a coast-to-coast TV news reporter, anchor, and talk show host.

When it came time for me to move on in my career, I thought back to how Cathy Martin motivated me to set a goal, to become all that I can be, to achieve my dream. I decided to take my broadcasting background and become a trainer and motivational speaker, sharing my secrets on how to make better presentations and enhance one's image, thus helping people to get the results they want by winning every audience. In essence, I became a coach. Once again, Cathy Martin's wisdom allowed me to achieve what I wanted to do. It all happened to me! Pushing through our fears and self-doubt can be a prolonged process or a simple decision. Cathy Martin taught me to decide—and to go for it.

Not long ago, a woman named Carol came to see me, seeking advice about the direction of her career. As I searched my mind for what would be most helpful to her at this important time in her life, Cathy Martin's words came flooding back.

"What do you want to do?" I asked her. Carol was ready to respond to the question. Proudly she told me, "I want to give talks to groups."

Acting unimpressed by her declaration, I asked, "What, specifically, do you want to speak about?"

"I'll speak on most anything uplifting."

"So will a lot of other people," I said sharply. "Speaking is a very competitive field. You need to know exactly what you want to speak about in order to succeed. You need to decide right here and now what it is you want to do."

Carol looked squarely in my eyes and stated with conviction, "I want to validate people's pain and make them feel better. I want people to love themselves and go for their dreams. I want to be a professional speaker giving talks on self-esteem."

I smiled. "Good," I said. "Now you know what you want to do. When you leave here, you tell everyone who you know what you want to do with your life—that you want to be a professional speaker who gives talks on self-esteem. And on those days when you're feeling uncertain, you share that uncertainty with your family, with your friends, with me. But as to the rest of the world, you address them with certainty in all that you do."

Carol left our meeting full of determination and confidence. Four years later, I learned she had become a sought-after professional speaker on self-esteem.

I can't help but wonder when she will pass on the invaluable advice my guidance counselor so generously shared with me so many years ago.

LINDA BLACKMAN

193

"Official" Hugs

ONE SUNDAY I PASSED HUG CARDS OUT TO THE CON-gregation. It may sound corny, but each of the Hug Cards reads: "Good for One Free Hug." While people laughed and made light of them, I witnessed person after person becoming softer and enjoying the process of giving to one another.

A shy Sunday-school teacher in the church works for the Internal Revenue Service. I've always pictured an IRS office as bureaucratic, gloomy, and cold, with mounds of paperwork. She noticed how all the hugging we did at church was good for us. When growing up, she was taught to be a private person. Years ago, if anyone had tried to hug her at church, she would have burst into tears of vulnerability and embarrassment. Not so today.

She wondered what would happen if she gave out Hug Cards at the IRS. On her birthday, she took in a whole stack of the "Good for One Free Hug" cards to work. After she had passed the cards around to each office, amazing things began to happen. People she recognized but had never met came from floors above and below her to ask if she was the lady who was giving out birthday hugs. A certain Bill even wanted to know if there was an expiration date!

Two years after the Hug Cards were introduced, a part-time em-ployee returned to work for the new tax season. And she was carrying her Hug Card! She said she had brought it along on her first day so she could be welcomed back to the office with a hug. Another employee, who was transferring to Colorado Springs, had saved his Hug Card, and he produced it on his last day to collect hugs from his IRS friends.

Bill, who had been especially enthusiastic about the card, later contracted cancer. When he retired early, not one person was embarrassed to give him a hug before he left.

It may be unusual to associate hugs with the IRS. Yet one person who was willing to take a risk clearly made a difference. People began thinking of themselves and of others differently. "Official IRS Hugs" became commonplace in her office.

Just think how our world would improve if we were all willing to hand out Hug Cards with no expiration dates and no conditions. The ripple effect of a hug would be much greater and last longer than an IRS refund check!

REV. MARY OMWAKE

❧

X

Tenderness and Compassion

⁂

"To keep a lamp burning, we have to keep putting oil in it."

—Mother Teresa

"We are not held back by the love we didn't receive in the past, but by the love we're not extending in the present."

—Marianne Williamson

Breaking Free

WHEN THEY CALLED MY NAME TO DISEMBARK AT THE Women's Federal Correctional Institute in Lexington, Kentucky, I was devastated.

The federal marshals grinned. Knowing I had believed I was being transferred from a maximum-security prison in California to a minimum-security camp in Bryan, Texas, they had purposely waited to call my name last. As I struggled down the steel steps of the aircraft in my shackles, my throat tightened, and I lost my voice. I couldn't blame the marshals—to them, I was just another inmate, a convicted felon.

Under armed guard, the other prisoners and I were led to a bus whose windows were caged over in chicken wire. It was April, but there was still a bite to the Kentucky air. I shivered, but only partly because of the cold. I knew Lexington was the most violent women's prison in the system. My mind remained stuck on one thought: Why, God? Why have you dropped me out of the palm of your hand?

I'd been in prison eight months. Following the pattern of most survivors of long-term sexual and physical abuse, I didn't know how to say no to my father when he asked me to commit fraud. I was convicted; he was not. I pleaded guilty and was given the maximum sentence allowed for my offense—twenty-one months.

When I had begun my prison sentence, I soon realized that the violence, the chaos, and the hypervigilance I was witnessing were simply reflections of what I had experienced throughout my childhood. I knew my life had to change. I asked for and was sent books of Truth, and I began writing affirmations. When I heard the voice of my father in my mind saying, *You are a nothing,* I replaced it with the voice of God saying, *You are my beloved child.* I wrote affirmations that didn't feel true but held the vision of what I knew to be true: that God loved me unconditionally and that I was a worthwhile person. Over and over, day after day, I began changing my life, thought by thought.

Arriving at FCI Lexington, I entered the dark night of my soul. I felt betrayed and frightened. What was the point of praying and affirming if I ended up in a worse situation than before? As the bus approached the gates of the prison, the twelve-foot double fences with razor wire on top were hints of what I would find inside the walls. I tried to pray. I really did. But all I felt was an immense sadness that once again, no matter what I did, nothing worked.

The guard who handled my paperwork commented, "You're here on an Infraction 313." I kept my head down, still not finding my voice. When I was strip searched and given my new uniform and bedroll, I was also handed a booklet of the rules and regulations of FCI Lexington. Quickly I turned to the back of the booklet, looking for the infraction numbered 313: "Lying or providing a false statement to a staff member." My heart began to pound even louder, for I knew I had been transferred for something I did not do. Once again, I felt trapped in a situation where I was powerless to convince others of the truth. After all, I knew there were only two rules between the guards and the inmates: one, inmates never trusted a guard, and two, guards never believed the word of an inmate.

As the women were led to their respective housing units, I noticed the units all had names reflecting the Kentucky outside the walls, such as "Bluegrass." One by one or in groups, all the inmates were turned over to the guards in the housing units, until finally there was just me. The guard led me to an elevator in the main unit, which housed the cafeteria and the commissary. I could not believe the huge number of women gathered both in the yard and in the unit. They pressed against each other and me. Many looked me over, some called and whistled to me. It was not friendly. The guard would not allow any other inmate in the elevator with the two of us, and for a brief moment I caught his eyes in fright. Would he hurt me? No, he just looked away. He gently pushed me off the elevator on the third floor, where he rapped loudly on a steel door. A guard came to let us in, and I marveled at the smallness of the unit. I saw only two women, and they were in wheelchairs. Where was I? The guard assigned me a room upstairs. I still had not spoken. I met several women on the stairs and heard the television blaring in the television room. I felt panic building inside, and only one thought sustained me as I climbed the stairs: "Get Gary on the phone."

My husband, Gary, had stood by me throughout the ordeal, totally supporting me in my recovery. He always believed in me, and in his eyes I was guilt-free. Instead of concentrating on my incarceration, Gary's letters and phone calls focused on the day I would come home to Kansas. He was my only link to the outside. Before I left California, I had called him with the good news that I was being transferred to Bryan, Texas. We were both excited, as we'd been able to see each other only once during my incarceration. In Texas, we could have regular visits.

There were five women and five iron beds in the room I was taken to. Dumping my gear on the one unmade bed, I turned to the woman in the bed closest to me and found my voice. "Where's the phone?" I demanded. She told me it was downstairs by the guard station. I left my gear on the bed and went back down the stairs, to wait an hour and a half for my fifteen-minute phone privilege. By the time Gary answered the phone, I was at a breaking point, and for the first time in almost a year, I cried. "I'm in Lexington, Gary!" I wailed. "And I think I'm going to die here!"

Gary had heard my stories of Lexington, passed on by inmates who were lucky enough to get transferred out. When he heard my voice, he began to cry too. He told me later he had never felt so helpless. I was in the hands of the federal prison system. "Don't cry, baby," Gary pleaded. "I can't do anything for you, but I can write to you. Look around and tell me the name of your unit, and I'll write to you tonight." Drying my tears, for I would not let another inmate see me cry, I stuck my head out of the phone booth and looked for a sign, such as "Bluegrass." Then I saw it. There, above the guard's station, was a simple sign that read: WELCOME TO RENAISSANCE. Slowly I began to smile, and I felt a warm rush of peace flow through me. I knew that no matter what the appearances, I was right where I was supposed to be. The "coincidence" of my unit being named Renaissance was a simple, clear reminder to me that I was still and always will be in the palm of God's hand. I was fine; I simply had more to learn. "Gary," I whispered, "it's OK. I'm going to be all right. The name of my unit is Renaissance—'Rebirth.'" I almost cried again, in joy. Gary calmed down somewhat in response to my voice, but our time was up, so I couldn't reassure him further. That would have to come later.

As I made my way back up the stairs, I knew God had not forgotten me, nor was I truly in the hands of the Federal Bureau of Prisons. I was right where I was supposed to be. I was safe. But suddenly I tensed. I realized I had breached an important rule in prison: I had been rude to my cellmates by not introducing myself to them before demanding the location of the telephone. Politeness and manners carry a very high priority in prison; with so many people crowded together, even a perceived lack of respect has an extreme price. I wondered if I would be facing my first fight at Lexington very soon.

As I stepped into the room, I noticed that someone had made my bed and that my clothes were missing. I looked at the woman in the bed next to mine. I should have known. When you have so little, even an extra pair of pants or a T-shirt has great appeal. I assumed the bed was made as an exchange for the clothes. I sighed and opened my locker, just to stall the moment of confrontation. I knew I would have to fight for my clothes.

But instead of an empty locker, what I found were my clothes neatly hung up, as well as a supply of toothpaste, deodorant, shampoo, and even lotion. The women in the room, who had so little themselves, had shared with me, who had even less. I bowed my head and smiled. I was more than safe; I was blessed. As I later learned, Renaissance is a medical unit for older and infirm inmates. Why I was sent there is still a mystery, since I was neither ill nor elderly. But I was safe. And that 313 infraction? The guard was mistaken. I had been transferred to be "closer to home." The Lexington facility wasn't as close to my home in Kansas as Bryan, Texas, would have been, but it was still a major improvement over California.

I introduced myself to the women in the room and thanked them for their generosity. None of them would admit to having given me anything. After taking a shower, I pulled back my sheets to get into bed and noticed one more act of kindness. One of the ladies had taken the time to baby-powder the sheets, making them silky instead of stiff and scratchy. I felt an overwhelming love build inside me and I thought: God, my God, you love me enough to have someone baby-powder my sheets.

I served the next five months in Lexington and was transferred to a halfway house in Kansas City to complete my sentence. I continued to study inspirational teachings and affirm the goodness I saw in myself and others.

When I finally came home, I asked Gary, "Do you see the changes, the life changes, I have made since I entered prison?" He responded, "No, what I see is the person I saw and knew to be there all along."

BARBARA ROGOFF

Grace

CHANGING THE WAY WE PERCEIVE INCIDENTS IN OUR life can change the way we respond to them.

A few years ago, I decided to add a ten percent grace factor in my life, and it has resulted in tremendous changes, all positive.

Assume a ten percent grace factor in your life:

Assume you'll pay ten percent more than your share of a dinner check shared with friends. Grace in your friendships is certainly worth that.

Assume that the bargain you got will cost ten percent less somewhere else tomorrow. Grace reduces stress.

Assume that you'll get cheated about ten percent of the time and that you'll lose about ten percent of your property one way or another. It costs to add grace to your life. It's worth it.

When you travel in another culture, assume a twenty percent grace factor. Then if you feel cheated by a taxi driver or someone else, it won't ruin more than a few minutes of your trip. Traveling in other countries requires grace.

Public grace will, in private, reduce tension, improve your perception of the world, improve your relationships, and increase your joy.

You'll end up with more of everything.

JENNIFER JAMES

Dedicated to Nealy

❦

I REMEMBER THE DAY WE WERE DRIVING THE HOUR'S distance down our country road, back from town and a day of errands. It was just my son, Alec, and I. We made small talk for a short time, then he leaned his head against the side window and rested. He was fourteen years old, and conversations with Mom no longer came easily.

Some time later, he startled me by breaking the silence. "Mom," he said, "I tried to pull her out of the way of the car, but I couldn't reach her in time."

My God, I thought, he still feels responsible for her death. "I know, Alec," I said. "It's not your fault."

He was referring to the night nine years earlier when Bill and I were out for dinner and the kids were home with a sitter. They were playing outside, and our two-year-old daughter was struck by a car near the house. Alec was closest to her and tenderly scooped her lifeless body into his arms, willing her to live. He held her for some time, but it did no good. The sitter called for help. In the panic and confusion, Alec's grandmother hastily yelled at him, "Why didn't you get her out of the way?" He just couldn't *think* why he hadn't gotten her out of the way.

The whole family did a lot of grieving and counseling. Alec and I hadn't spoken of her in a long time. I assumed that after all this time, he had worked it through.

Now I realized that no amount of "It's not your fault" comments from me or the counselor had relieved Alec's mind. Oh, God, I thought, I cannot face her death again. The pain is too deep. And yet here's Alec sitting across from me, still filled with guilt and self-blame. His pain is still living and breathing in his mind, eating away at his heart. He had taken on the responsibility for a tragic accident that was not his fault. I didn't know what I was going to do, but I made the commitment to do *something*.

The next morning, my conversation with Alec was still fresh in my mind as we drove by our local grade school. Suddenly I got an idea. I asked Alec to go with me into the kindergarten classroom, to observe for a while. He couldn't figure out why I wanted him to come with me.

"So we can learn about responsibility," I said.

When we walked into the room, the kids were busy painting, coloring, and pasting.

I noticed Alec's expression when we walked into the room. His look seemed to say, "I'm a fourteen-year-old guy . . . what am I doing here?" Very quickly, however, I noticed his eyes soften, and he began to take notice and delight in the kids' laughter and innocence.

Easing into the conversation, I said, "Alec, would you ask that little girl over there to help you with your homework?"

"No, Mom. She's just a kid," he replied.

"Well, maybe we should ask Tommy over there to run to the store for us. I'm starved."

"Come on, Mom," he said. "He's not old enough to do that."

"Well, if one of the children in this room had an accident and was dying, would you expect that another child could prevent the child's death?" I asked.

"Mom, a kid can't do that," Alec said without thinking.

"Alec, you were five years old when Nealy had a horrible accident. I know that you were in no way responsible for that accident, and no one, not even you, could have saved her. What's more important is that you now know that too."

Alec looked at me for a time without saying a word. The realization of what he had just learned for himself was sinking in: he was not responsible for Nealy's death. A new kind of peace washed over my precious young man.

SUSAN P.

Hot Dog! Thou Art!

❦

I WAS EIGHTEEN YEARS OLD, AND I WAS THE GOLDEN girl. A junior in college, I was president of the college drama society, a member of the student senate, winner of two off-Broadway critics' awards for acting and directing, and director of the class play. In class, my mind raced and dazzled as I tossed off quick answers in class and impressed my teachers and fellow students. Socially, I was on the top of the heap. My advice was sought, my phone rang constantly, and it seemed that nothing could stop me.

I was the envy of all my friends, and I was in a state of galloping chutzpah.

The old Greek tragedies warn us that when hubris rises, nemesis falls. I was no exception to this ancient rule. My universe crashed with great suddenness. It began when three members of my immediate family died. Then a friend whom I loved very much died suddenly of a burst appendix while camping alone in the woods. The scenery of the off-Broadway production fell on my head, and I was left almost blind for the next four months. My friends and I parted from each other, they out of embarrassment and I because I didn't think I was worthy. My marks went from being rather good to a D-plus average.

I had so lost confidence in my abilities that I couldn't concentrate on anything or see the connections between things. My memory was a shambles, and within a few months I was placed on probation. All my offices were taken away; public elections were called to fill them. I was asked into the adviser's office and told that I would have to leave the college at the end of the spring term, since clearly I didn't have the "necessary intelligence to do academic work." When I protested that I had had the "necessary intelligence" during my freshman and sophomore years, I was assured with a sympathetic smile that intellectual decline such as this often happened to young women when "they became interested in other things; it's a matter of hormones, my dear."

Where once I had been vocal and high-spirited in the classroom, I now huddled in my oversize camel's-hair coat in the back of classes, trying to be as nonexistent as possible. At lunch I would lock myself in the green room of the college theater, scene of my former triumphs, eating a sandwich in despondent isolation. Every day brought its defeats and disacknowledgments, and after my previous career I was too proud to ask for help. I felt like Job and called out to God, "Where are the boils?" since that was about all I was missing. These Jobian fulminations led me to take one last course. It was taught by a young Swiss professor of religion, Dr. Jacob Taubes, and was supposed to be a study of selected books of the Old Testament. It turned out to be largely a discussion of the dialectic between Saint Paul and Nietzsche.

Taubes was the most brilliant and exciting teacher in my experience, displaying European academic wizardry such as I had never known. Hegel, gnosticism, structuralism, phenomenology, and the intellectual passions of the Sorbonne cracked the ice of my self-doubting, and I began to raise a tentative hand from my huddle in the back of the room and ask an occasional hesitant question. Dr. Taubes would answer with great intensity, and soon I found myself asking more questions.

One day I was making my way across campus to the bus, when I heard Dr. Taubes addressing me: "Miss Houston, let me walk with you. You know, you have a most interesting mind."

"Me? I have a *mind?*"

"Yes, your questions are luminous. Now, what do you think is the nature of the transvaluation of values in Paul and Nietzsche?"

I felt my mind fall into its usual painful dullness and stammered, "I d-don't know."

"Of course you do!" he insisted. "You couldn't ask the kinds of questions you do without having an unusual grasp of these issues. Now, please, once again, what do you think of the transvaluation of values in Paul and Nietzsche? It is important for my reflections that I have your reflections."

"Well," I said, waking up, "if you put it that way, I think . . ."

I was off and running, and I haven't shut up since.

Dr. Taubes continued to walk me to the bus throughout that term, always challenging me with intellectually vigorous questions. He attended to me. I existed for him in the "realest" of senses, and because I existed for him, I began to exist for myself. Within several weeks, my eyesight came back, my spirit bloomed, and I became a fairly serious student, whereas before I had been, at best, a bright show-off.

Dr. Taubes acknowledged me when I most needed it. I was empowered in the midst of personal erosion, and my life has been very different for it. I swore to myself then that whenever I came across someone "going under" or in the throes of disacknowledgment, I would try to reach and acknowledge that person as I had been acknowledged.

I would go so far as to say that the greatest of human potentials is the potential of each one of us to empower and acknowledge the other. We all do this throughout our lives, but rarely do we appreciate the power of empowering others. This gift can be as simple as "Hot dog! Thou art!" Or it can be as total as "I know you. You are God in hiding." Or it can be a look that goes straight to the soul and charges it with meaning.

I've been fortunate to have known several of those the world deems "saints": Teilhard de Chardin, Mother Teresa of Calcutta, Clemmie, an old black woman in Mississippi. To be looked at by these people is to be gifted with the look that engenders. You feel yourself primed at the depths by such seeing. Something so tremendous and yet so subtle wakes up inside that you are able to release the defeats and denigrations of years. If I were to describe it further, I would have to speak of unconditional love joined to a whimsical regarding of you as the cluttered house that hides the holy one.

Saints, you say, but the miracle is that anybody can do it for anybody! Our greatest genius may be the ability to prime the healing and evolutionary circuits of one another.

JEAN HOUSTON

Ritual: a tradition, a time-honored practice; a rite.

Tootsie Roll Ritual

RITUALS ARE A WONDERFUL WAY TO CONNECT WITH those I love. Meaningful rituals provide predictability, stability, and roots.

My favorite childhood ritual occurred at my grandfather's house. As a young girl, I would get to Grandpa's farmhouse, scramble out of the car, throw open the front door, and race, as fast as my little legs would carry me, to the pantry at the back of the house. There I would wait excitedly. Tall and lanky Grandpa Schulte, always dressed in his striped bib overalls, would slowly and silently stroll to the pantry as well. He'd reach high up on a shelf, take down the "magic" box, and, with a big smile, stoop down to my level. I would reach in and grab as many Tootsie Rolls as my little fists could hold. This unconditional offering was symbolic to someone growing up in a house with five brothers. Everything in my life seemed to have limits. Grandpa's Tootsie Rolls were an exception.

Dad often remembered the wonderful relationship he had with his grandfather. He remembered how he had watched me run to his father to collect fistfuls of Tootsie Rolls. Now that I was grown and married, he longed to be the revered grandpa, handing out the Tootsie Rolls.

When I became pregnant with my first child, I carefully wrapped a package to send to my dad. I lovingly placed it in the mail.

I was told my father wept with surprise and joy when he opened the package. It contained a box stuffed with Tootsie Rolls.

MARY LoVERDE

"Imagination is the highest kite one can fly."

—Lauren Bacall

Waste Not, Want Not

ONE YEAR IN THE LATE FIFTIES, MAMA CROCHETED OUR Christmas—neck scarves, berets, and mittens. We raised Angora rabbits in chicken-wire cages kept in the garage; from their fur Mama made our gifts.

I remember the Saturday a large package arrived from Sears Roebuck. It was a spinning wheel. While the five of us kids listened to our favorite radio shows—the Nelsons, the Green Hornet, the Lone Ranger —Mama spun the fur into thread.

"Just imagine how warm the angora will keep the children this winter," she said to Papa.

"The way you dress them, I'm afraid they'll die of *underexposure*. You haven't let them build up a lick of resistance," Papa said, teasing.

Parents of the fifties suffered two world wars, a depression, and Korea. They were frugal and conservative and squandered little. "Charity begins at home" was a slogan, as was "Waste not, want not." I remember Mama always borrowing from Peter to pay Paul. It was a long time before I knew who those fellows were.

When Mama died this past June, I found myself drawn into a tunnel

214

of childhood remembrances. Strange things surfaced, like the taste of the Denver mud Mama applied to my chest when I had a cold. She heated the mud in the lid on the burner, then spread it on my chest. To ward off the evil spirits of virus and bacteria, she made us take cod-liver oil potions. Our lips were greasy with fish lard and our breath smelled like seafood for hours.

We saved money every way possible, which meant that Mama acted as our nurse and our doctor. In a past life, I think she was a medicine woman, a shaman, or a witch. She had a cauldron of remedies. Papa worked out of town, inspecting power lines. The pay was poor, but both he and Mama wanted us to have nice things like other kids. They did the best they knew how, cutting corners and skimping on things.

One Monday, the year after we received our neck scarves and mittens, I found Mama staring and twisting her thumbs as she sat in the old pink rocker.

"What's wrong, Mama? "

"Just worried about Christmas. There's no extra money for gifts, I'm afraid."

Traditionally on Monday nights we gathered around Mama and Papa's bed and prayed the rosary. Mama suggested we ask for God's help. We gathered in the bedroom, gripping our rosary beads. "A family that prays together stays together," she said.

It didn't seem like our prayers were heard, for the next day our Philco upright radio went on the blink. Now we wouldn't be able to listen to our shows. Most of the neighbors had black-and-white televisions, but it would be another two years before Papa would buy us a little portable TV. We sat around at night playing blackjack, Monopoly, and Chinese checkers. Sometimes we fought, accusing each other of cheating. All of us were edgy about Christmas, but I've always had a lot of faith and truly believed in the power of prayer. I held tight to the image of a magical Christmas morning—everyone would have gifts.

On the weekends, Papa came home, and he and Mama held conferences. When they weren't conferring, Papa was in the garage, tinkering. I knew he could do some things well, but often his ideas were less than professional. Once, installing a light switch in the kitchen, he put the box on the outside of the wall instead of the inside. Another time, he invented an automatic dog feeder, which he wanted to patent. Dog food rotated on conveyor belts. I never understood the point. On the patio we had an old car-seat chair with pipes for legs—Papa's idea of constructing furniture.

From Friday night, when he came home from work, until Sunday afternoon, when he left, he was in his shop. This went on for weeks. We were all curious. The clock ticked: Christmas is coming—Christmas is coming. Then finally it came.

I was the first one up. We'd decorated the tree the night before, with tinsel, glass balls, and bubble lamps. I plugged the lights in and lay on my stomach, looking at the few gifts that were under the tree. I'd been saving my allowance and had a package of razor blades wrapped for Papa and some stockings for Mama. I gave my brothers marbles—bought one sack and divvied them up. My sister would get a new headband. I felt good about having gifts for everyone. While I counted packages, my sister slipped into the room.

"What's that?" she said, rubbing her eyes.

"What's what?" I asked.

"That," she said, pointing to a huge *something* in the corner of the living room, covered with a sheet.

"I don't know," I said.

At the unveiling. my sister and I gasped. Under the sheet was the most beautiful dressing table and stool we had ever seen. An antique mirror was attached to the back. It had cubbies for our barrettes and bobby pins, and there was even a drawer in the stool. We were thrilled. This is what Papa had been doing in the garage. In a strange way, I felt I knew this piece of furniture, that it belonged. The boys had homemade toolboxes and their own sets of tools from Papa's spares. Mama had a new coffee table, the top made from old black and white ceramic tile that had been stored in the garage.

All day, my sister and I took turns sitting at the dressing table, putting on lipstick and earrings and brushing each other's hair. I remember running my hand along the smooth polished wood, almost embracing it. This was the best gift ever—an answer to my prayers for a magical Christmas. When my sister dropped a bobby pin, I bent over to pick it up and noticed some gold writing on the side of the dressing table. It read *Philco*.

LINDA ROSS SWANSON

Intensive Caring

AS A CRITICAL CARE NURSE, I KNEW FROM YEARS OF experience that the scene before me was not a hopeful one. There was no movement, no audible breath sounds. IV poles surrounded him like so many pencil-thin trees, offering their various fluids in hope of sustaining life. I read his chart and noted that he was no longer responding to the efforts of medicine. Now, as he lay here in the ICU, it was only a matter of time until his body was put to rest.

Slowly, I walked around the bed. I was somewhat preoccupied with my thoughts about the finality of life, medicine, life supports, and dying. I methodically labeled all the IV tubes, so that I knew which bottle led to which arm with what medication. Deep in thought, I barely heard her walk in. She gave no sign that she even saw me as she quickly walked to the bedside, leaned over, and smoothed the man's hair. I immediately felt like an intruder in a very private relationship.

"Any change?" She smiled as she asked, not looking at me but keeping her gaze on the man.

"I wish I could say yes." I watched as she took one of his hands and eased herself down in the chair next to him, never abandoning her vigilance on his unresponsive face.

"How long has it been since you were able to hold each other?" I had to ask. Her longing was so great that my question seemed not intrusive but necessary.

"Too long," she said, tears following the familiar path down her face. "It was so sudden. His heart . . ." Her sobs ended the sentence as she moved even closer to the bed.

"Would you like to hold him? Would you like to gather him into your arms and cuddle? Is your relationship close like that?"

For the first time, she looked at me. Curious, hopeful, and self-conscious. A sob escaped with her answer. "Yes, I would love to hold him."

I quickly moved to the bedside, arranged tubes, bags, and machines, then motioned to her. Hesitantly she came to my side, and then she slipped cautiously into the small bed beside her husband.

Then I became self-conscious, an uninvited witness to their intimacy. I quickly turned my back and pulled the curtains partway around the small cubicle, enclosing them in a private space.

As I busied myself with nursing duties, I could hear her murmuring sweet nothings, reassuring him, reassuring herself, and unknowingly reassuring me. I turned to readjust an IV drip and caught a glimpse of her running her fingertips gently down his cheek, then softly kissing him.

I didn't try to hide my tears as I helped her out of the bed and held her close. "I miss him so much," she whispered. "I've wanted to hold him for so long that I ache. We have always cuddled and been close. I *knew* he wanted to hold me one more time too. . . . Thank you."

Not long after, while she sat holding his hand, his spirit left to go on its journey.

Once more, I held her.

PATTY ROSEN

ↈ

XI

Learning to Laugh at Ourselves

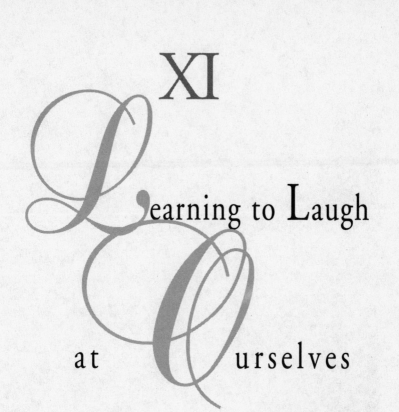

"*Don't get your knickers in a knot.*
Nothing is solved,
and it just makes you walk funny."

—Kathryn Carpenter

The Last of the Big, Big Spenders

IVE DOLLARS AND FIFTY-NINE CENTS. . . .

"Ma'am! That will be five dollars and fifty-nine cents," said the young thing with the big hair standing behind the cash register at McDonald's. She tapped her chrome-plated, inch-long nails on the counter in annoyance. She was the perfect counterpart to the foil message draped behind her: "Joy to the World! Happy Holidays!"

I dug through my purse. I hadn't intended to stop here for dinner, but my five-year-old son had insisted.

"Let's see, five and fifty, five and fifty-five, five and fifty-eight . . ." I held my palm out to her, imploringly. From behind me, a man tossed a penny onto the counter.

Alms for the poor? Hey, OK. Anything to speed the process along.

Balancing the tray on one hand, I navigated to the table already staked out by my son. With the ease of a veteran McDonald's habitué, he opened the box, located the holiday-theme toy, and began to munch his way through thousands of calories' worth of greasy, salty french fries. Two fistfuls later, he nonchalantly wiped his hand down the front of his clothes and announced, "I gotta go to the bathroom." Hence the name "fast food."

But today I didn't worry about the effects of fast food on my son's digestive system. Today I was on Cloud Nine, because the night before, I had hosted the perfect Christmas party. I moved through McDonald's in dreamy reminiscence of the triumph I had enjoyed just last evening. Last night I had done the impossible, the suburban wife's Olympian feat: the flawless, Martha Stewart, eat-your-heart-out Christmas party.

223

"You realize we must show our new members the heights to which they can aspire," Myrtle, the hospitality committee chair, had said to me in early November. "Seeing a veteran member who has, well, *made it* gives them added commitment to our organization." She had paused to sniff delicately, then added in a whisper, "I am sure they will be very, very impressed by your . . . hospitality."

And they were. By December 15, the house was spotless, dressed in its holiday finest. By sheer force of will, and great planning, I had even managed to groom myself to the max before the first dinging of the Westminster chimes from the doorbell.

Usually, my modus operandi consists of sliding through the foyer and snatching frantically at the door, while pulling up sagging panty hose with my spare hand. Halfway through past galas, I would manage to sneak away and reappear with makeup, a trick that always causes the heavy drinkers to cut back.

But not last night. Last night I appeared before the first guest as the hostess with the mostest, immaculately dressed, cool, and calm. Last night was snooty, snobby perfection.

I tossed the tray contents into the trash receptacle and steered Michael to the john. As he dried his hands under the blow dryer, he turned to me and said, "I can't wait to go back and finish my food. I'm really, really hungry."

Oops! The food was in the garbage. Michael began to howl.

"I'm hungry! I'm starving! And my toy is gone too. *Aaauuuuuhhh!*" He raised his voice several decibels.

"Well . . . I don't have any money," I said quietly and desperately.

He howled, "Get me my *foooood!*"

I made an executive decision. I reached into the trash. Fishing around frantically, I pulled up a half-eaten burger, a handful of lettuce, and a Happy Meal box. I peered inside. Yep, it was his. I turned to hand it to him and looked up into the face of Myrtle, standing silently beside another genteel woman.

"Goody good," said Michael with glee. "I'm so, so hungry."

Myrtle smiled thinly. Her lipstick was on slightly crooked, I noted with satisfaction as I picked a wilted piece of lettuce off my wrist.

"Oh, Joanna, I was just telling Mrs. Freeman here about your home. It is so . . . so . . ."

"Elegant? Expensive?" I supplied, stuffing the lettuce into the trash.

"Yes . . . oh . . . uh," and Myrtle's gaze shifted to my son and his burger.

The woman beside Myrtle was entranced. Rarely have I seen anyone so stunned. She and Myrtle stood there quietly, waiting for the beads of perspiration to form as I tried to explain my predicament.

I decided to deny them the pleasure.

"Well, my dear departed mama always said that if you look after the pennies, the dollars will take care of themselves. Come along now, Michael. We have other trash cans to explore. Mama is a little hungry herself."

JOANNA SLAN

◈

Coats That Don't Fit

ƏƖₚ

I WAS INVITED TO FLY IN A HELICOPTER TO AN OFF-shore oil rig. I had never been in a helicopter, and I definitely had never been on an offshore oil rig. I tried to control my excitement. I arrived hours early at the Lompoc airport. Eventually about twenty of us were milling around, most of them men who work on the rig. These big, burly guys are called roustabouts.

Our tour guide arrived. Or should I say drill sergeant? He immediately ordered us outside for the weigh-in. Weigh-in? When I signed up, no one had mentioned a weigh-in. The only kind of weigh-in I undergo takes place in the far north corner of my closet, where I have hidden my scale and a flashlight. There, all alone, I turn on the flashlight, zoom the room to make sure there are no spies, weigh myself, and get out of the closet fast. Now, that's my kind of weigh-in.

Hoping not to be noticed, I attached myself to a group of roustabouts, and we walked outside. When I saw the scale, I knew I was in trouble. It sat in the middle of the runway and had a platform so large we could have all done a rip-roaring square dance on it. The arrow pointing to the pounds was at least six feet tall. Our drill sergeant shouted, "Jack Nife, step up on the scale." Uh-oh. Jack Nife was number one on the sign-in log, I was number four. I had a very short time to figure out how I was going to weigh in without anyone noticing where the arrow landed. That familiar voiced shouted out, "Patsy Dooley, step right up."

Without a moment's hesitation, I jumped up on that scale, grabbed an imaginary mike, and began singing "Let me entertain you, let me

226

see you smile," as I did a fast two-step shuffle across the scale. I jumped off the other side and bowed. From the expressions on their faces, I knew that none of them had paid any attention to that arrow in the sky. Some of them, however, were no doubt reconsidering going on this adventure with me.

The drill sergeant handed us lifesaving-type coats. When I put mine on, I knew right away I had a problem. It didn't fit. After several abortive tries to zip my coat, I decided, "Oh, pooh, I'll just wear it *casual.*" Our drill sergeant began to inspect the troops. When he got to me, he stopped abruptly. "All coats must be zipped and secured before anyone boards this helicopter." He shouted so loud that I was sure everyone on the offshore oil rig knew I was coming—and I was coming with an *unzipped zipper!*

Determination set in, but no amount of scrunching, tugging, pulling, mental imaging, or praying was going to make that coat fit. Finally, I pulled the bottom of the coat up around my neck. I huffed and puffed as I inched the coat down from my shoulders, and engaged the zipper. It was like crawling into a girdle backward! I was so busy, I didn't notice that a group of guys who work the rig had surrounded me. As I manipulated the zipper, they reached up, grabbed the bottom of the coat, and yanked. I was poured into the coat. I could not bend. I could not breathe. Lack of oxygen was causing my brain to become somewhat rattled. My heart, liver, and corpuscles were all busy meeting each other. The guys cheered. I couldn't get a cheer out.

The drill sergeant then announced that tucked up inside the back flap of the jacket was a thing called the "diaper." In case of an emergency, we were to bend over, reach up between our legs, unsnap the "diaper," pull it through our legs, and snap it to the front of our coats. My eyes locked in on the drill sergeant. He must have seen my panic, because a hint of mercy seemed to appear in his eyes. He cleared his throat. "Normally, we practice this maneuver," he bellowed. Then he looked at me. Everyone looked at me. "But I think we'll skip it this trip." Everyone sighed. I could not sigh. I was having this mental picture of my roustabouts, who had formed an emotional responsibility for my well-being, circling me in the water, trying to assist me with my diaper, as we all went down for the third time.

However, thanks to a little help from my friends, all went well that day. It took me a while to see the humor in the situation, but eventually I could look back and laugh as hard as my roustabouts had. What a spectacle I must have been, trying to get into that coat.

Later, as I thought about it, I was able to see an analogy. Changes in our lives usually feel like my lifesaving coat did, tight and uncomfortable. Whether the change is marriage or divorce, a baby or a graduation, a new job or a layoff, it is uncomfortable at first, and we all struggle. Sometimes, however, when the struggle seems especially intense and lonely, God sends "roustabouts." They hug me when I cry. They pick me up when I fall. They cheer as I make changes and congratulate me when I stick to my goals. Each new "coat" has been good for me. I've grown through the struggles and have been blessed because of the roustabouts in my life. Because of them, I can continue to put on coats that don't fit.

PATSY DOOLEY

SP

Fifty Is Nifty

ON MY FIFTIETH BIRTHDAY, MY OLDER DAUGHTER GAVE me a pin that said: 50 IS NIFTY. I wore it to work that day, and what fun it was! All day, people kept saying things to me like, "Anita, you don't look fifty " or "Why, Anita, you can't be fifty" and "We *know* you can't be fifty."

It was wonderful. Now, I knew they were lying, and they knew I knew, but isn't that what friends and coworkers are for? To lie to you when you need it, in times of emergency, like divorce and death and turning fifty.

You know how it is with a lie, though. You hear it often enough, and you begin to think it's true. By the end of the day, I felt fabulous. I fairly floated home from work. In fact, on the way home, I thought: I really ought to dump my husband. After all, the geezer was fifty-one, way too old for a young-looking gal like me.

Arriving home, I had just shut the front door when the doorbell rang. It was a young girl from a florist shop, bringing birthday flowers from a friend. They were lovely. I stood there holding the flowers and admiring them, and the delivery girl stood there, waiting for a tip.

She noticed the pin on my jacket and said, "Oh, fifty, eh?"

"Yes," I answered, and waited. I could stand one last compliment before my birthday ended.

"Fifty," she repeated. "That's great! Birthday or anniversary?"

ANITA CHEEK MILNER

"The way I see it, if you want the rainbow,
you gotta put up with the rain."

—Dolly Parton

A Wise Old Sage

ON AN EXCEPTIONALLY TRYING SUNDAY EVENING, I HAD
been responding to the temperamental mood swings of my son, Eli.
Although Eli is thoroughly charming, he is also a typically willful
five-year-old. It had clearly been a day of power struggle, as he gave
new meaning to the phrase "difficult child." I had bitten the bait far
more times than I care to admit.

I've read those books designed to shape the ultimate parent. I have
vowed to achieve the totally unnatural responses they advocate. To be
the Unpushable-Button Mother has been my goal. For most of that
day, it worked.

Perhaps nothing more than my own exhaustion roused me by his
bedtime. If I could just get him into bed and make it downstairs, I
knew everything would be all right again. I could return to the safety
and security of my high-pressured career in the morning—with significant relief!

I can't recall exactly when my brilliant little negotiator finally shoved
me over the edge. Maybe it was the request for yet another glass of

water. Or just one more book. Or his urgent need to locate a tiny Lego aqua shark he had not played with in over a month. But out it flew, loud and clear: "Eli, *just shut up!*"

I turned in anger, fleeing to the sanctuary of my favorite reading chair in the living room. I was thoroughly beaten and disgusted with myself. With my adrenaline flowing, I was certain there should be laws against people like me becoming a mother! (So *this* is how women lift cars off their children! Or drop them onto them, depending.)

Ten minutes later, as calmness and sadness settled where fear and anger had been, I opened my eyes to find a quiet visitor at my feet. As Eli climbed into my lap, he leaned forward and said gently, "I want to whisper something to you."

Anticipating an endearment, I held him close. "What . . . you . . . said . . . wasn't . . . very . . . nice," he informed me. His tone was paced and deliberate, with a touch of sass that said I'd been nailed.

Welcoming his honesty, I agreed.

"You're right, sweetheart, and I'm sorry. I try *never* to say words like that, because they hurt your feelings. I was feeling angry, tired, and upset, but that's no excuse. Can you forgive me?"

With a nod of his head and a grin, he leaned against me for a five-minute cuddle. I watched him relish his middle-digit "suckie finger" on his left hand. So hard to be five . . . one moment a wise old sage, the next a little babe again. No wonder they're tormented creatures.

Back in his bed, sitting bolt upright with his legs extended in the way only small children can achieve, he glanced at me sideways with his characteristic sparkle.

Experience should have cued me, but I never saw it coming. Eli fluffed his covers onto his lap, smiled his sweetest smile ever, and put our hellish Sunday to bed. "Well, Mama, it's good we had this discussion tonight."

JACQUELINE GILLIS ELLIOTT

◈

Preserving Miz Wells

ഗ്ര

F THERE'S ONE THING WE GREEKS LIKE TO DO, IT'S eat. We also like to cook, which is why some ninety percent of Greek immigrants to the United States open restaurants.

My grandmother arrived in Virginia as an immigrant bride in 1900, which meant there was not a single person she could talk to in her city except for her husband. The language barrier created a second, even more desperate, problem. She could not invite other women over for tea so that she might show off her prowess in the kitchen. In desperation, she had six children.

When her second daughter, Connie, began school, Grandmother's chance to invite a guest for food suddenly materialized. Connie had a fight in the second grade with a little boy, and the teacher, Miz Wells (that's the Virginia pronunciation) confronted her. "Well, Connie, just go home and tell your mama I'm coming to see her at four-thirty this afternoon."

Connie rushed home and announced the impending visit. Grandmother received the news with a mixture of joy and terror. Here, at last, was someone she could stuff to death. With two hours' preparation time, she flew into a frenzy. She threw a baklava into the oven, sliced a ham, brought out a wheel of cheese, and dipped thirty olives out of brine into a bowl. This would be for the main serving, which comes after a respectable length of time.

The first serving—the best homemade preserves you have—is presented the moment the guest enters the door. By tradition, the preserves are piled generously into a bowl in show-off fashion, even if only one guest is expected. Along with them come a spoon and a glass of iced water, so that the guest can take one helping, hold it over the water, and eat it. In the back of the tray are six to eight small glasses filled with homemade wines and brandies. The guest takes her choice.

Grandmother's preserves, brought from Greece, were candied green walnuts in a rich and powerful syrup. One walnut would last you several weeks. Two could kill you.

When Miz Wells arrived, Grandmother admitted her and shouted (because you always talk louder to foreigners), *"Seet down."* Then she rushed to the kitchen and returned with the preserve tray. She shoved it under Miz Wells's chin and ordered, *"Eat!"*

Miz Wells whimpered, "Well, ah don't know if ah kin eat all this, but I certain'y will try!" And she picked up the bowl and ate all twenty-two of the preserved green walnuts. As Grandmother watched in stunned silence, her guest then drank the water. Dazed, Miz Wells regarded the small glasses and asked, "What's in all these li'l glasses?"

Down went the ouzo. The seven-star brandy followed. After she consumed the remaining six firewaters, she walked stiff-legged to the door. She never called again, and Grandmother formed her opinion of American educators that afternoon. "Bunch of drunks, coming in here and eating everything in the house!"

HOPE MIHALAP

❧

Head Majorette

O N ONE OF MY MORE SELF-ASSURED DAYS IN MY THIR-teenth year, I volunteered to be the head majorette for our small-town drum-and-bugle corps, the Applearrows. Although I had not yet mastered the art of baton twirling and stumbled during marching drills, I rationalized that my gymnastic abilities well qualified me for this prestigious position. Did I mention that I was also arrogant?

The big parade day arrived, and I proudly began flipping, cartwheeling, and marching my band along the crowded parade route. Family, friends, and even favorite teachers had come to cheer me in my new endeavor. This was a rare mountaintop experience for me; and I was savoring every aspect of this dream come true.

Suddenly I felt a frantic tap on my shoulder and heard an irritated voice in my ear. It was my band director. He spun me around just in time for me to see the disappearing backs of my band members as they marched two blocks away in the other direction.

Lessons I learned that day:

1. Don't take yourself too seriously.

2. It takes more than guts and arrogance to be a leader.

3. A good leader looks over her shoulder now and then to make sure the "arrows" are pointing in the right direction.

4. However fast you run, it's really hard to catch up with a group that is marching in the opposite direction!

CANDIS FANCHER

More Chocolate Stories?

Do you have a short story that fits the spirit of *Chocolate for a Woman's Soul?* I am planning several future editions, using a similar format. One will feature love stories of all kinds, while another book will focus on inspirational stories emphasizing a magical moment in life. I am seeking heartwarming stories of two or three pages in length that feed and lift the spirit, help us to learn about life, and tug at our emotions.

I invite you to join me in these future projects by sending your special story for consideration. If your story is selected, you will be listed as a contributing author, and you may include a biographical paragraph of your choice. You retain the right to use your story for other purposes, and I will have a onetime right to publish it. For more information, or to send a story, please contact:

KAY ALLENBAUGH

P. O. Box 2165
Lake Oswego, OR 97035

Contributors

Burky Achilles is a writer and recipient of a Walden Fellowship. She is working on her first novel as well as a book of inspirational short stories. She and her husband are raising a daughter and a son on the brink of teenhood. (503) 638-4100.

Emory Austin, Certified Speaking Professional, was recently featured in *Industry Week* magazine, along with fellow speakers Colin Powell, Margaret Thatcher, and Terry Anderson. She is a Phi Beta Kappa Communications graduate of Wake Forest University and has keynoted in almost every industry, to rave reviews. For information regarding Emory's presentations and tapes, please call (704) 663-7575.

Ursula Bacon fled Nazi Germany with her parents and spent the next nine years in China. She was interned along with 18,000 European refugees by Japanese occupation forces in Shanghai for four years. She emigrated to the United States at the end of World War II. Ursula is married to author Thorn Bacon, and they operate a small publishing house and write books. She is the coauthor of *Savage Shadows* and the author of *The Nervous Hostess Cookbook.* (503) 682-9821.

Maggie Bedrosian, MS, business owner and executive coach, specializes in helping people produce focused results with natural ease. Author of three books, including *Life Is More Than Your to Do List: Blending Success & Satisfaction,* Maggie hosted television's *Spotlight on Business.* She is past president of the American Society for Training &

Development, Washington, D.C., chapter. Audiences enjoy her light-hearted programs at business gatherings, or on cruise ships, and at the Disney Institute. (301) 460-3408.

Linda Blackman, a consultant, trainer, and professional speaker, shows executives how to make more effective presentations to all audiences and teaches company spokespersons the secrets of handling the media. She is a former coast-to-coast TV reporter, anchor, and talk show host. Linda knows how to transfer the power of the spoken word to you. (412) 682-2200.

Joan Borysenko, PhD, is the president of Mind/Body Health Sciences, Inc., and the author of several books, including *Fire in the Soul,* a *New York Times* bestseller; *Minding the Body, Mending the Mind;* and *Guilt Is the Teacher, Love Is the Lesson.* She cofounded and is a former director of the Mind/Body Clinic at New England Deaconess Hospital and was an Instructor in Medicine at Harvard Medical School. One of the architects of the new medical synthesis called psychoneuroimmunology, Dr. Borysenko is herself a cell biologist, a licensed psychologist, and an instructor in yoga and meditation. (303) 440-8460.

Mildred Cohn graduated from college with honors at age sixty-eight. She resides in Fort Lauderdale, FL.

Wendy Craig-Purcell is the senior minister at the Church of Today in San Diego, CA. Wendy was a skater with the Ice Capades before becoming the youngest ordained minister in the Unity movement. Her ministry is characterized by her personal strength and an attitude of open and unconditional acceptance. (619) 689-6500.

Patsy Dooley is a humorist and motivational speaker who thrives on challenges and change. Through her twenty-five years in the business world, she creates funny and value-packed programs to show people how to add humor to their lives. Her gift of connecting humor with reality, and of sensing business climates, affords a fresh originality to her programs. She brings her own unique stories and humor for her audiences' enjoyment and growth. (805) 489-1091.

Kay duPont, Certified Speaking Professional, is executive vice president of The Communication Connection, an Atlanta company that custom designs communications and relationship programs for organizations all over the world. (770) 395-7483.

Edith Eva Eger, PhD, an Auschwitz survivor, is a licensed psychologist and a keynote speaker, workshop leader, and consultant. She tailors her presentations to the unique requirements of business, government, military, health care, religious, civic, community, and educational organizations. Dr. Eger's unforgettable presentations bring dynamic new perspectives to the universe of human behavioral issues facing all people and organizations today. (619) 454-8442.

Shirley Elkin, MSEd, is a professional speaker and trainer based in Decatur, IL. She presents keynotes and leads seminars on Body Language in the Business World, Change Your Thinking—Change Your Life, and Professional Presentation Skills. She has a master's degree and worked in secondary education prior to becoming a speaker and trainer. (217) 875-1721.

Jacqueline Gillis Elliott is a freelance writer living in West Linn, OR. She received her master's in physical therapy in 1977. Positions she has held include therapist, consultant, university instructor, rehabilitation manager, and director of quality services. She credits her husband, Dave, her son, Eli, and many geriatric clients with contributing healing doses of humor and inspiration to the most ordinary moments of daily living.

Christine B. Evans, MA, a marriage and family therapist, has been in practice for twenty-three years in Sebastopol, CA. She is a keynote speaker and leads women's support groups and workshops on shame and empowerment. She wrote *Breaking Free of the Shame Trap: How Women Get into It, How Women Get Out of It.* John Gray, author of *Men Are from Mars, Women Are from Venus,* says of her book, "An important and strong book and a necessary support for validating women's feelings at a time when it is most needed." (707) 829-5901.

Candis Fancher, MS, CCC in Speech Pathology, is the founder of Inner Sources. Her well-known "Pleasure Pause" seminars energize participants to adopt more positive lifestyles. Her inspiration came from her own life-threatening illness and the loss of a family member. She sees the immediate benefits of integrating humor into patient care. Her clients include hospitals, professional organizations, public agencies, and commercial businesses. (612) 890-3897.

Eleanor S. Field, PhD, is a licensed psychologist, marriage and family therapist, and hypnotherapist in private practice in Tarzana, CA. She is the coauthor of *The Good Girl Syndrome* and has participated in many radio and television interviews, including *Donahue, Hour Magazine,* Tom Snyder, and Michael Jackson. Dr. Field is on staff at the Encino-Tarzana Regional Medical Center and consults on pain control and depressive disorders. She is a member of the National Speakers Association and speaks on motivational topics and "The Mind-Body Connection." (818) 708-3559.

Fran Fisher is a Certified Personal and Professional Coach and president of Living Your Vision, which provides guidance and coaching for individuals and small-business owners. "We each have a unique divine design that desires to be fulfilled," says Fran. She blends the art of visioning, the structure of planning, and her intuitive ability to help clients fulfill their heart's desires. (800) 897-8707.

Carolyn Fox is currently writing a book about her spiritual and personal growth from her motorcycle adventure through all fifty states. (514) 957-5631.

Edwene Gaines is a Unity minister known for her life-changing seminars such as: Prosperity Plus Workshop; Integrity, Commitment, Riches and Honor; Rites of Passage; The Firewalk; and Celebrating the Goddess Within. For a list of her tapes and materials, contact: (800) 741-6790.

Patricia Forbes Giacomini is a freelance writer residing in Denver, CO. (303) 733-7220.

Lola D. Gillebaard lives in Laguna Beach, CA. A recipient of the Reader's Digest Writers Award, she is a professional speaker and a past president of the Greater Los Angeles Chapter of the National Speakers Association. Her one woman show, *Life's Funny That Way,* has been acclaimed all around the country. Lola is a humorist, a college associate professor, an author, and a corporate keynoter. She believes that laughter is the handshake of good communication and that humor in business is serious business. (714) 499-1968.

Lynne Goldklang, MA, MFCC, is a psychotherapist in private practice in Los Angeles. She gives seminars on humor and healing and is coauthoring a book, *Count It as a Vegetable and Move On,* all about stressing less and enjoying life more. (213) 874-5097.

Ann V. Graber (aka Westermann) is a gifted counselor. She holds a Master of Divinity in Interfaith Ministerial Counseling and earned her Diplomate in Logotherapy from the Viktor Frankl Institute of Logotherapy. As a consultant/educator, Ann works with individuals and groups using meaning-centered therapeutic approaches. Her inspiring audiotapes, *Images of Transformation,* are available by calling (314) 947-6175.

*P*am Gross is the founder and vice president of CareerMakers, a life-planning and career management firm in Portland, OR. She is the author of *Want a New, Better, Fantastic Job? (The How-to Manual for the Serious Job Seeker).* Pam Rollerblades, swims, reads theology and fiction, and enjoys hiking in old-growth forests. (503) 244-1055.

*D*onna Hartley is a motivational, informational speaker. She is known for *Fireborn—9 Skills for the '90s,* her true-life story, featured on PBS, and for her *Get What You Want* video series. She can be reached at (916) 581-2005.

*K*athlyn Hendricks, PhD, ADTR, has had a lifelong passion for transformation and the power of consciousness. She directs the Hendricks Institute, which conducts trainings and workshops in relationship and body-centered transformation throughout the United States and in Europe. She is the coauthor of nine books, including *Conscious Loving* and *At the Speed of Life,* and has appeared regularly on national television with her husband and partner, Gay Hendricks. (805) 565-1870.

*J*an Hibbard has a background in social services and real estate and is presently marketing wellness products for Nikken International. She lives in Portland, OR, with her husband and two children. (503) 244-5752.

*C*onnie Hill is founder and president of The Fulfillment Center, Inc., a service company that provides organizations with warehousing services to distribute and fulfill requests for product and literature. Hill started The Fulfillment Center in 1988 with $100 and one client. Today she operates a 15,000-square-foot facility and has twenty-five clients. Hill lives with her husband and two teenage boys in San Rafael, CA. (707) 224-6161.

*J*ean Houston, PhD, is an internationally known psychologist, scholar, philosopher, and teacher, who has developed revolutionary ways of unlocking the latent human capacities existent in each human being. The author or coauthor of over fifteen books—including *Public like a Frog; Life Force; The Possible Human; Godseed; The Search for the Beloved;* and *The Hero and the Goddess*—she has also worked in human and cultural development in over forty countries. Her school of spiritual studies, modeled on the ancient mystery schools, is now in its twelfth year. (914) 354-4965.

*B*arbara Marx Hubbard is an author and a world-renowned futurist, social innovator, speaker, citizen diplomat, social architect, and prophetic politician. She has led a life of perseverance and commitment to a single purpose: To understand, communicate, and encourage the evolutionary potential of humanity. Barbara has written *The Hunger of Eve; The Evolutionary Journey;* and *The Book of Co-Creation: The Revelation: A Message of Hope for the New Millennium.* With her partner, Sidney Lanier, she has cofounded the Foundation for Conscious Evolution. For information, call (415) 454-8191.

*S*haron Hyll, DC, is a chiropractic physician in private practice in Saint Louis. She focuses on chronic disease management, integrating body, mind, and spirit into her practice. Acupuncture and nutrition are also extensively used. She lives with her husband, two stepchildren, two cats, one dog, and two Volvo wagons. (314) 256-7616.

*K*imberly Jacobsen is Planning Director for Wasco County, OR, and a mother. (514) 298-5169.

*J*ennifer James, PhD, holds a doctorate in cultural anthropology and master's degrees in both history and psychology. She is a columnist for the *Seattle Times* and one of Seattle's most popular commentators. A renowned lecturer worldwide, she is the author of five books, including *Success Is the Quality of Your Journey,* which has sold over 100,000 copies. (206) 243-5242.

*B*erniece Johnson, who is not a contributor but who is featured in the story "Angel on Patrol," is a police officer. She aspires to be the first black female country singer. (503) 240-4917.

*A*pril Kemp, MS, is an award-winning motivational speaker and sales trainer. She is dynamic, with a high-energy delivery style dedicated to the education of audiences nationwide. Her company specializes in motivational keynote speaking and teaching women the art of selling. Along with her husband, April developed a motivational software product, Motivational Mind Bytes™. (800) 307-8821.

*M*arlene L. King has an MA in art therapy (cum laude). She is executive vice president of Exhibitron Corporation and co-owner of FutureQuest Co. She writes, edits, and conducts seminars and classes in the field of dreamwork. Her dream-based oil paintings have been shown at Planetfest, Illuminarium Galleries, and Northwoods Galleries. She is a member of the Association for the Study of Dreams and the American Art Therapy Association. (541) 471-9337.

*K*athy Lamancusa, CPD, CCD, MSF, writes and presents Family Lifestyle, Creativity, and Creative Skills programs designed for parents, teachers, and students. Over one million copies of her books and videos have been sold, her column appears in magazines nationally and internationally, and she can be seen on television on the Discovery Channel, the Learning Channel, PBS, and Home & Garden Network. Her own show, *At Home with Flowers,* is a "how to" lifestyle program appearing on PBS around the country. For information on seminars, presentations, books, and videos, call (330) 494-7224.

*G*ladys Lawler is a ninety-three-year-old poet living in Kansas City, MO.

*I*rene B. Levitt, MGA, an instructor and professional lecturer in handwriting analysis at the college level since 1985, is president-elect of the National Speakers Association, Arizona chapter. She provides document examination, vocational analysis, criminal investigation, jury screening, and personality assessments. She is an expert on grapho-therapy and is working with inner-city teenagers to help improve their self-esteem. She is a member of the Governors' Commission on Prevention of Violence Against Women. To order her book, *Brainwriting,* or the audiotape/booklet *A Key to Your Personality—Using Handwriting Analysis,* call (602) 661-9199.

*M*ary LoVerde, MS, ANP, is a professional speaker and founder of Life Balance, Inc. Her passion is researching new ways to balance career success with a happy and healthy family. She has produced an audiotape series entitled "June Cleaver Never Fried Bacon in a Bill Blass Dress" and is the author of the book and videotape *Your Family's Greatest Gift,* soon to be published. (303) 755-5806.

*P*hyllis Mabry has published poetry and articles during her twenty years teaching in secondary education. She serves as a writing judge for the National English Council and is currently working on her first novel. (217) 428-1166.

*A*nn McGee-Cooper, EdD, author, lecturer, business consultant, and creativity expert, is a widely recognized leader in the emerging field of brain engineering. Her work has been featured in such major publications as the *Chicago Tribune, USA Today,* and *International Management.* She has authored three books, *Building Brain Power, You Don't Have to Go Home from Work Exhausted!* and *Time Management for Unmanageable People.* Her Creative Time Planner is now available through Day-Timers. She can be reached at (214) 357-8550.

*M*ary Jane Mapes, Certified Speaking Professional, professional keynote speaker and seminar leader, specializes in interpersonal communication and managing personal change. She is known for thought-provoking, cutting-edge programs that appeal to the head and touch the heart. She is from Kalamazoo, MI, and can be contacted by calling (616) 324-1847.

*D*anielle Marie, entrepreneur, business consultant, and author, acts as a Chief Imagination Officer on many boards, helping companies grow creatively. In her book, *Straight from the Heart,* authors, celebrities, and others share their philosophies on making a difference in the world. The book inspires readers to see how we all can make a difference. (602) 368-8526.

*S*helly Marks, MS, is coauthor of *Miscarriage: Women Sharing from the Heart.* (619) 469-6267.

*A*lex Merrin is an intuitive personal growth coach, whose passion is supporting people in conscious evolution. A senior associate of the Hendricks Institute, she is director of the institute's Personal Supervision Program, working with individuals, couples, and corporations. (503) 228-7784.

*C*onnie Merritt is a writer and a humorous and engaging professional speaker, who speaks in fifty cities a year on dealing with difficult people, change, and building your business. She is currently working on three books, *Finding Love Again: The Over-Forty Dating Survival Manual; Ten Smart Conversations to Make Your Marriage Work;* and *Tame the Lions in Your Life: Dealing with Difficult People and Tough Times.* (714) 494-0091.

Hope **Mihalap** is an author, an actress, and a radio personality, and is the voice behind hundreds of national commercials. As a professional speaker, she has received the prestigious international Mark Twain Award for Humor, won also by Bob Hope and others. She is one of only twenty women in the world to be awarded the National Speakers Association's Council of Peers Award of Excellence. She has an ear for accents and an eye for hilarious situations. (804) 623-0429.

Susan **Miles,** a photographer and writer, is currently studying for a degree in art therapy. (503) 282-6266.

Anita **Cheek Milner** is a lawyer, a humorist, and a stand-up comic. She enrolled in law school in her forties, passed the California bar exam at age fifty, and is now known as "The Change-of-Life Attorney." Anita keynotes to groups all over the United States, presenting "Laugh and Stay Healthy." (800) 747-9130.

Jann **Mitchell** is a feature writer for *The Oregonian* in Portland. She has received national awards for her coverage of social issues, features, humor, and mental health. Her popular Sunday column, "Relating," provides insights into our relationships with others and ourselves. She is the author of four books: *Codependent for Sure; Organized Serenity; Home Spiritual Home;* and *The Holiday Survival Guide.* She also lectures frequently on self-development. (503) 221-8516.

Mary **Manin Morrissey** holds a master's degree in psychology. Her growing global audience is a tribute to her inspirational speaking and teaching ministry. She counsels and leads seminars reaching thousands each year as founder and spiritual leader of the Living Enrichment Center, often referred to as a model of the 21st Century Church. She is the author of *Building Your Field of Dreams.* (503) 682-5683.

*M*arguerite Murer is an educator, a professional speaker, and an inspirational writer. Her keynote addresses, seminars, and workshops are noted for their electrifying interaction and explosive insights. (817) 273-5234.

*W*endy Natkong works as a paramedic in Juneau, Alaska. A freelance writer, she is currently working on her second novel. (907) 789-7825.

*S*heryl Nicholson is the president of her own consulting firm, More Than Survival! "Gifts of the Heart" is an edited excerpt from her seminar, published in April 1991 in *Esteem*. She can be reached at (813) 684-3076.

*M*ary Omwake has been the senior minister of Unity Church of Overland Park in Kansas since 1989. Under her leadership, the congregation has grown from under 200 to 1,500 members. Prior to attending ministerial school, Mary received a BA in psychology from California State University, Irvine, and completed her graduate work in education at the University of California. The church's Outreach Program has reached more than 2,500 children, inner-city adolescent girls, and gang members; it also provides care to 2,500 adults in nursing homes and abuse shelters. (913) 649-1750.

*R*osita Perez, author of *The Music Is You*, has received the Council of Peers Award for Excellence, was named Speaker of the Year by the National Management Association, and has been given the two most coveted awards from the National Speakers Association. She changed careers at forty, when she picked up her guitar and decided she could do meaningful, life-transforming programs by using music and self-disclosure from the platform. Her commonsense approach and use of humor have led to her being described as a "revitalizer" at national conventions around the world. (352) 376-0133.

*P*enelope Pietras is a freelance writer and editor in Colorado. She conducts memoir-writing workshops and is currently working on a novel. (303) 791-3981.

*D*iann Roche is an agent for commercial artists and photographers. Although based in Kansas City, she represents these talented people on a national level. Diann's goal is to bring integrity and peace to every person she meets or with whom she speaks. (816) 822-2024.

*B*arbara Rogoff is a writer and cocreator of the workshop for adult survivors of abuse "Beyond Survival into Triumph." She has a prison ministry that incorporates techniques to quiet the chaos, find hope in the present moment, and thereby attain personal freedom. She lives in Stilwell, KS, with Gary, her husband and best friend of nineteen years. (913) 897-7250.

*P*atty Rosen is a writer, lecturer, facilitator, consultant, and Nordic ski instructor. She was formerly a registered nurse and certified nurse practitioner, and was clinical director for a chapter of Planned Parenthood and Urban League Family Planning. She sponsored the Oregon Death with Dignity Ballot Measure. (541) 389-7280.

*H*arriet Roth, MSEd, is an infant massage instructor through the International Loving Touch Foundation, Inc. She draws from twenty-eight years' experience as a kindergarten and first-grade educator with a master's degree in education as well as an Early Childhood Certificate. Harriet has a passion for teaching children. (503) 520-0352.

*M*ary Murray Shelton is senior minister of the Huntington Beach Church of Religious Science in southern California, and is dean and director of the Holmes Institute: A Graduate School for Consciousness Studies. A minister since 1986, she currently serves on the International Board of Trustees for the United Church of Religious Science. Originally trained in theater, she uses storytelling as one of the ways to bring messages of truth into real-life terms for our everyday living. (714) 969-1331.

*J*oanna Slan is a mother, wife, and professional speaker. She may be found at better trash cans near you or onstage, presenting to large and small groups of people. Joanna speaks on topics she has yet to figure out, like balancing one's life, communications, having fun, and peacefully coexisting with difficult people. Meanwhile, keep your eyes open for Joanna's book, *If Mama Ain't Happy, Ain't Nobody Happy: How Women and Their Families Can Live Life with More Joy and Less Stress.* (800) 356-2220.

*J*ody Miller Stevenson, author of *Soul Purpose* and *Soulutions,* draws from twenty years' experience teaching thousands of people nationally how to "discover their unique and special purpose for existence." Her specialty is assisting others to create and manifest their personal vision while mastering the transition process. Her delight is coaching people as they awaken to their potential and their personal passion. Jody is currently a counselor in private practice, speaking nationally and leading seminars on creative expression. (503) 977-2235.

*S*uzy Sutton, Certified Speaking Professional, is a speaker, trainer, and entertainer. A working actor in film and TV commercials, she produced and hosted the Philadelphia radio and TV show *We Can't Stop Now* for sixteen years. She is the author of *Practical Steps to Speaking Up and Out,* and the coauthor of *Build a Better You.* (215) 493-4766.

Linda Ross Swanson is a freelance writer who frequently publishes essays and poetry. "Waste Not, Want Not" is an excerpt from her upcoming book, a collection of essays and vignettes about life with her manic-depressive mother. (503) 292-4755.

Mari Pat Varga is a professional speaker and workshop leader who specializes in interpersonal communication, presentation skills, and peak performance. Mari Pat has inspired, entertained, and challenged business audiences since 1985. (312) 989-7348.

Acknowledgments

MY HEARTFELT THANKS GO TO THE CONTRIBUTORS OF this book. Their individual and collective enthusiasm and their willingness to tell their favorite uplifting stories created the beauty herein.

Many thanks and the warmest regards to my agent, Maureen Walters, and my editor, Becky Cabaza, for the ease with which this project flowed. My deep gratitude goes to my review board: Clara Harwood, Ginny Warren, and Phyllis Weter. Their love of the project, their support of me, and their objectivity brought a unique perspective and individual "taste" to the stories they felt would have the most impact on readers. The stories they helped select represent a cross section of inspirational experiences important to women from around the country.

I would also like to thank: Patty Rosen for her friendship and beautiful editing; motivational speakers Maggie Bedrosian, Joanna Slan, Linda Blackman, and April Kemp for their encouragement and suggestions; writer Penny Pietras for her ability to add tenderness to a story; Mary Omwake and Barbara Rogoff, where it all began. Special thanks go to Kathie Borstel, Linda Kemp, Marilyn Guldan, Ursula Bacon, Carole Greenberg, Karen Howells, Janet Reigel, Cathy Kinnaird, Karen Weight, M. J. Evans, Debbie Rosas, and Rev. Bruce Robinson for their support, feedback, and friendship. Thanks to my family—especially to Dad, for being interested enough to read every story!

Not all of the hundreds of stories contributed are in this book, but they all touched my heart. Here are a few women I want to pay special tribute to:

- Jane Adams lost her twelve-year-old daughter, Susan, in a tragic automobile accident. Six years later, she was invited to speak at the high-school graduation ceremony for Susan's class. This invitation allowed Jane the opportunity to be Susan's mom one more time on a more positive note.
- Diane Hunsaker is no stranger to hardship. She lost both her parents as a young girl. Diane learned that *determination* makes the difference in getting something done. Once married, with a family of her own, Diane longed to attend college. She returned to school while working full time. Diane attended classes for fourteen years—one hour per day, during her lunch hour! She graduated recently at age fifty, and is now in a master's program —this time attending night classes.
- Sandra "Kandy" Mandel was in the process of writing her story when she died of cancer. Her courage, compassion for others, and sweet spirit are sorely missed by all who knew her.

Applause to my husband, Eric. His clarity of direction, vision, and values continue to be an inspiration to me. He is my life partner and my teacher. Thank you, Eric, for your belief in, encouragement of, and love for me.

The greatest reward from compiling this book has been the new friendships of sixty-eight women from around the country. I respect and admire their work, and I'm honored to have their stories in *Chocolate for a Woman's Soul*.

Permissions Acknowledgments

"A Legacy of Love" is an edited version of "A Mother's Unexpected Legacy of Love." Reprinted from *Miracles* magazine with permission of Joan Borysenko, PhD.

"Hot Dog! Thou Art!" is an excerpt reprinted by permission of The Putnam Publishing Group/Jeremy P. Tarcher, Inc., from *The Possible Human* by Jean Houston. Copyright © 1982 by Jean Houston.

"Flower Power" is an excerpt from *The Music Is You*, Knox Publications, with permission of Rosita Perez, CPAE.

"Gifts of the Heart" is an edited excerpt from *Esteem* magazine, with permission of Sheryl Nicholson.

"Thanks for the Miracle, Sis" is reprinted from the "Relating" column, *The Oregonian*, with permission of Jann Mitchell.

"Grace" is a reprint from *Success Is the Quality of Your Journey*, Newmarket Press, with permission of Jennifer James, PhD.

About the Author

KAY ALLENBAUGH IS A FREELANCE WRITER AND PUBlicist. She lives with her husband, Eric, in Lake Oswego, Oregon.